Healing is for You!

Maria Vadia

Hans Yattwald
534 - 8765

Queenship

PUBLISHING COMPANY
P.O. Box 220 • Goleta, CA 93116
(800) 647-9882 • (805) 692-0043 • Fax: (805) 967-5133
www.queenship.org

Bibles used:

All scripture references taken from the Holy Bible, Revised Standard Version, Catholic Edition, unless indicated otherwise.

The Holy Bible, Revised Standard Version, Catholic Edition. Ignatius Press, San Francisco. 1966.

The New American Bible, Saint Joseph Edition. Catholic Book Publishing Co., New York. 1970.

The Holy Bible, New King James Version. Thomas Nelson, Inc., Nashville. 1982

© 2007 Queenship Publishing - All Rights Reserved.

Library of Congress Number # 2007923685

Published by:
   Queenship Publishing
   P.O. Box 220
   Goleta, CA 93116
   (800) 647-9882 • (805) 692-0043 • Fax: (805) 967-5133
   www.queenship.org

Printed in the United States of America

ISBN: 1-57918-332-8

Dedication

It's my desire that all who are sick and hurting in any way may have an encounter with Dr. Jesus to receive the healing He already bought for us on Calvary. I pray that your minds be renewed to believe that the Lord wants you well in spirit, soul and body. According to Jeremiah 29:11, He has plans for you, "plans for welfare and not for evil, to give you a future and a hope."

Thanksgiving

I want to thank our precious Holy Spirit and the Catholic Charismatic Renewal for restoring this truth of healing to the church, and all the faithful "little people" who continually pray and lay hands on the sick and suffering for healing and deliverance. You are doing the works of Jesus, be encouraged and expect more!

Table of Contents

Healing is for You!

I have good news! If you are a child of God, healing is for you, because it's part of the inheritance that Jesus won for you on Calvary. In Isaiah 53: 4-5 it says:

> "Yet it was our infirmities that He bore,
> Our sufferings that He endured,
> While we thought of him as stricken,
> As one smitten by God and afflicted.
> But He was pierced for our offenses,
> Crushed for our sins,
> Upon Him was the chastisement that
> Makes us whole,
> By His stripes we were healed." (NAB)

On the Cross Jesus carried every sickness and disease so that you could be healed today. You can receive healing and wholeness because He already obtained your healing 2,000 years ago on Calvary. This is part of your inheritance. He not only dealt with the sin of humanity, but also with every sickness and disease, with every emotional lesion or hurt you could be carrying. This is awesome! The Lord has already made your healing available. It's there waiting for you! Don't ignore this wonderful benefit from the Cross of Jesus Christ!

> "Bless the Lord, O my soul,
> And forget not all His benefits,
> Who forgives all your iniquity,
> Who heals all your diseases…" (Psalm 103:2-3).

Let us pray:

> "Father, I thank You for Your perfect and complete plan of salvation for my life, which includes healing for my entire being, spirit, soul and body. Holy Spirit, Spirit of revelation, show me my inheritance and help me to appropriate my healing. Jesus, my Lord and Savior, I want to know You as my healer and to trust You for my health and healing. Amen."

Foreword

Maria Vadia's book on physical healing accomplishes three things for the believer:
1. Brings Jesus' intent for healing to the reality of every believer's life.
2. Interprets scripture, old and new testament in a practical loving way to show God's plan for healing from the beginning.
3. Invites us as 'ordinary' believers to the 'praying' field, teaching us how easy and rewarding it is to obey the command of Our Lord.

This is a work for new believers for every back ground, seasoned intercessors lay people and clergy alike will be renewed in their faith, and Catholics who have been taught that healing no longer occurs.

Evangelist Vadia, by sharing her testimony, encourages us to new levels of faith in the promises of the gospel, while disciplining us in the ways of 'ordinary' Christianity.

We are challenged to get off the bench and into the market place bringing this very exciting truth to our every day life. This work will bring courage to the faint hearted who have been struggling with the age old questions, 'what did I do to deserve this illness?' Is it God's will for me to be healed? And how do I pray for healing?

The author leaves no stone unturned as she addresses many issues fraught with controversy including generational and inner healing, occult involvement, and forgiveness.

You will be challenged to action, and revived to new spiritual heights.

This is reality Christianity in the that reality TV can never be. Missionay-Evangelist Maria Vadia draws you into the warm water of living in the spirit by sharing her loving relationship with her Abba Father. The result of obedience is the almost palpable abiding presence of Jesus Himself... The result of her obedience promised... "abide in me, and I will abide in you."

For those of us already involved in the healing ministry, this work serves as a refreshing revival, reminding us that Jesus is no respecter of persons, that His love for his people hasn't changed, and neither has his command to 'go ye therefore.' For those who have never considered the possibilty that Jesus heals today, it's a wonderful wake up call.

For those who are 'pew potatoes,' waiting to see how the reality series ends, it's a drink of new wine, which will probably lead to a desire and thirst, for righteousness.

Whatever your situation, you will be enlightened, encouraged, and entreated by this author's 'get out of the boat' style. The Holy Spirit has used Ms. Vadia's work to bring the old and new testament together in the life blood of Jesus our Savior in a way that makes us want this life to be lived through us. She shares her life and work with such a humility and insistence that everyone can do this, that you will feel compelled to test the waters for yourself.

Cheryl Williams
Christian Healing Minisries, Inc.
Prayer Ministry Corrdinator

Introduction

When I was a child I read a lot. I think I loved every book… unless I had to write a book report. Then I really hated the book because I was so afraid I wouldn't say all the right things, to make sure some teacher really knew I read the book. This is the first time I have been asked to write an introduction for a book. I am honored to be asked. The task terrifies me…another book report, sort of.

My only solution is to reflect on the message as I heard it and pass that on in a few words. I trust that the Lord will take this overweight arrow, and with His power shoot it into hearts to germinate stem, flower and leaf. I hope you can see even the smallest portion of the encouraging and challenging and joyful message that Maria Vadia awakened for me. She will say it was the Lord. She is right. But she also says that if we would but allow ourselves to come into His presence, He will work in ways unimagined. Maria gave me an opportunity to get excited about the possibility all over again. She helped me recall places where the Lord has been in my life, and she also encouraged and challenged me to have no less an expectation for tomorrow. That is the job description of a true disciple.

Sometimes, one person's way of saying something is another person's distraction – perhaps like this "book report." Let Maria do what she does so well: let her lay out before you the richness of Scripture. It is the Lord's word. And He never distracts, only invites. Seek Him here.

Father Jim Fetscher, Pastor
St. Louis Catholic Church
Miami, Florida.

I

Healing is Your Inheritance!

PAPA WANTS YOU WELL!

"Beloved, I pray that all may go well with you
And that you may be in health; I know that it
Is well with your soul." (3John:2).

It's God's desire that we be in health; spirit, soul and body. This is why He made provision for our healing through the death of His Son Jesus on the cross. This is why the Holy Spirit gifts us with gifts of healing; this is why Jesus commanded us to lay hands on the sick. This is why when Jesus commanded His followers to preach the Gospel it went accompanied with a command to heal the sick:

Matthew 10: 1 "And He called to Him His twelve disciples and gave them authority over unclean spirits, to cast them out, and to heal every disease and every infirmity."

Matthew 10: 7-8 "And preach as you go, saying, The kingdom of God is at hand." Heal the sick, raise the dead, cleanse the lepers, cast out demons. You received without pay, give without pay."

Mark 6:12 "So they went out and preached that men should repent. And they cast out many demons, and anointed with oil many that were sick and healed them."

Healing is for You!

Mark 16: 15-18 "And He said to them, 'Go into all the world and preach the gospel to the whole creation... And these signs will accompany those who believe: In My name they will cast out demons; they will speak in new tongues;...they will lay their hands on the sick, and they will recover.'"

Luke 9:1-2 "And He called the twelve together and gave them power and authority over all demons and to cure diseases, and he sent them out to preach the kingdom of God and to heal."

Luke 10:8 "Whenever you enter a town and they receive you, eat what is set before you; heal the sick in it and say to them "The kingdom of God has come near to you."

I think Jesus meant business when He commanded His disciples to heal the sick. It was not a nice suggestion, but a command. He didn't even tell His disciples to pray for the sick; He commanded to heal them! It is the power of the gospel in action! The Apostle Paul says in 1 Corinthians 4:20 "For the kingdom of God does not consist in talk, but in power." The gospel is to be demonstrated not only in its power to convict and bring repentance, but also to heal and set people free from bondage. Amen!

Sickness and disease were not part of God's plan for humanity. They entered humanity through the sin and rebellion of Adam. In His mercy for us, God sent His son Jesus to "destroy the works of the devil" (1John 3:8) so that we could be saved, healed, delivered and restored. Jesus Himself spent a great deal of time healing the sick; He had great compassion for the sick and hurting. He saw sickness as an enemy, something that needed to be destroyed. Why did He do that? Because it was His Father who commanded Him to do it. How do we know that?

Jesus said to them, "Truly, truly, I say to you, the Son can do nothing of his own accord, but only what He sees the Father doing;

for whatever He does, that the Son does likewise." (John 5:19). Jesus only did what the Father showed Him to do; so the fact that Jesus healed the sick meant that it was exactly what the Father wanted. He was an obedient Son! As a matter of fact, there are two things that the Lord commands us to do when we enter a home: release the peace of the kingdom in that household and heal the sick there. Luke 10: 5 & 9 says:

"Whatever house you enter first say, Peace be to this house! ...heal the sick in it and say to them, The kingdom of God has come near to you."

According to Jesus, one sign that the kingdom of God has come near is the healing of the sick!

The first revelation of God to His people after they crossed the Red Sea was the revelation that God was their healer. This is important for us to understand; after the Israelites were delivered from slavery in Egypt, crossed the Red Sea and saw their enemies drowned and defeated, the Lord revealed Himself as their healer:

"...for I am the Lord, your healer." (Exodus 15: 26).

This is a revelation of His nature and character. We too have been forgiven and delivered by the Blood of Jesus out of the hand of the enemy, and by the triumph of the Cross our enemies have been defeated. Healing comes next! First we have the revelation of Jesus as being our Savior and Deliverer from sin, bondage and satan, then comes the revelation of Him as our healer. "Bless the Lord, O my soul, and forget not all His benefits, who forgives all your iniquity, who heals all your diseases." (Psalm 103:2-3). First He deals with the iniquity, then comes the healing. We cannot ignore the healing ministry of Jesus; it is so dear to His heart!

In the book of Ezekiel 34: 4, we see how the Lord was grieved because the people in authority in those days did not heal His sheep:

Healing is for You!

"The weak you have not strengthened, the sick you have not healed, the crippled you have not bound up, the strayed you have not brought back, the lost you have not sought..."

Healing was included for God's people in the Old Testament; if healing was included in the Old Covenant of the law, imagine today that we are under a superior covenant, the New Covenant of His blood! Hebrews 8:6 says "But as it is, Christ has obtained a ministry which is as much more excellent than the old as the covenant He mediates is better, since it is enacted on better promises." So we see that the Lord Jesus has obtained for us a "much more excellent" covenant with "better promises." Healing is included in this covenant; we need it to fulfill His plan and purpose for our lives in this planet. We want to live a long and fruitful life, extending His kingdom and giving Him glory until He calls us home!

"As He went ashore He saw a great throng; and He had compassion on them, and healed their sick." (Matthew 14:14).

Healing is Your Inheritance!

JESUS THE HEALER

"...how God anointed Jesus of Nazareth with the Holy
Spirit and with power; how He went about doing good and
healing all that were oppressed by the devil, for God was
with Him." (Acts 10:38).

Everything that Jesus did was a reflection of what the Father was
doing; He never disobeyed His Father. He said "I always do the
thing that pleases Him" (John 8:29). Jesus said "My food is to do
the will of Him who sent me, and to accomplish His work" (John
4:34). If Jesus healed the sick it's because He was obeying the
Father. Jesus said in John 5:19-20,

"Truly, truly, I say to you, the Son can do nothing of His
own accord, but only what He sees the Father doing; for
whatever He does, that the Son does likewise. For the
Father loves the Son, and shows Him all that He Himself is
doing...."

Some people believe that it is God who sends disease; if that
is the case, then Jesus was a disobedient Son because He spent
so much time healing the sick! However, we know that Jesus
never sinned (Hebrews 4: 15). He "went about doing good and
healing..." He came to bring abundant life (John 10:10) and "to
destroy the works of the devil" (1John 3:8).

Jesus had a passion to heal the sick. Jesus was so committed to
healing, that when He healed on the Sabbath it even brought great
persecution against Him from the religious authorities, but He did
it anyway because it was the will of the Father to heal on that day.
After Jesus healed a sick man on the Sabbath (John 5:1-18), John
writes that "this was why the Jews persecuted Jesus, because He
did this on the Sabbath." In Mark 5: 1-6, Jesus healed a man with
a withered hand in the synagogue. It was on the Sabbath. The
religious authorities were so upset that "The Pharisees went out

and immediately held counsel with the Herodians against Him, how to destroy Him." When Herod threatened to kill Jesus, some Pharisees advised Him to leave the city. Jesus replied: "Go and tell that fox, "Behold, I cast out demons and perform cures today and tomorrow, and the third day I finish my course." (Luke 13: 31-32). In other words, Jesus basically told them, "I will continue to carry on with deliverance and healing, which is what I'm supposed to be doing now until the crucifixion." No one could stop Jesus from doing what He came to do: healing was one of the things He came to do. As simple as that!

Another example of the compassion of Jesus for the sick is this. After learning of John the Baptist's death, His desire was to withdraw to a lonely place, but something unexpected happened (Matthew 14:13-14):

"Now when Jesus heard this, he withdrew from there in a boat to a lonely place apart. But when the crowds heard it, they followed Him on foot from the towns. As He went ashore he saw a great throng; and He had compassion on them, and healed their sick."

We see from this passage how Jesus healed the sick even when He had plans to be by Himself. It seems that sick people never turned him off, but rather He was always ready to receive them and heal them. He knew by revelation that it was His Father bringing them to Him.

In Matthew 21:12-16, in the midst of Jesus cleansing the temple and driving out all the merchants and money-changers, "the blind and the lame came to him in the temple, and he healed them." Jesus was just amazing! One minute He's overturning tables and seats, but when He sees the sick coming to Him, He stops everything He's doing to heal them!

During the Passion, on the night He was arrested (Luke 22:51), Jesus even took time to heal the high priest's servant's ear. This is

just amazing!
Today if you're in need of healing, know that today He still heals. The Lord didn't send you that disease! Go to Him! Jesus hasn't changed and He doesn't suffer from mood swings! He's still the Healer!

"Jesus Christ is the same yesterday and today and for ever." (Hebrews 13:8)

Healing is for You!

THE GOSPEL:
THE POWER OF GOD TO HEAL

"For I am not ashamed of the gospel: it is the power of God for salvation to every one who has faith...." (Romans 1:16).

The gospel of the kingdom is not just a bunch of nice words; it's the power of God to forgive, save, heal, deliver, restore, make whole. It's really good news! That's why Paul was not ashamed of it. The Greek word used for salvation in this passage is the word "soteria." This word means not only forgiveness, but wholeness, deliverance, general well-being. It includes the person's total well-being. Healing is included in the "salvation package." Another word used for "salvation" in the New Testament is the word "sozo" (Luke 7: 50). It means saved, healed and delivered. The Apostle Paul writes to the believers in Rome:

"But I know that when I come to you, I shall come in the fullness of the blessing of the gospel of Christ." (Romans 15:29) (NKJ).

The Apostle Paul wanted every believer to experience "the fullness of the blessing of the gospel of Christ." He did not despise any of the blessings of the gospel; he wanted God's people to receive all the blessings of the kingdom. Healing is a blessing of the kingdom! Jesus told His disciples in Luke 12:32

"Fear not, little flock, for it is your Father's good pleasure to give you the kingdom."

If we really understood that the kingdom is ours and that Jesus Himself teaches us to pray to the Father "let Your kingdom come, let Your will be done on earth as in heaven," we would be expecting "the fullness of the blessing of the gospel of Christ," which includes healing, to be released in us and through us today. We saw in the previous chapter how Jesus' command to His disciples to preach the gospel went accompanied with the command to heal the sick. The early Church followed in the footsteps of Jesus. They preached everywhere and there were miracles, healings, resurrections, signs and wonders that followed His followers. Let's look at some of the healings:

✦ Acts 3: the healing of a man who was lame from birth; this miracle brought 5,000 converts to Jesus.

✦ Acts 5: 15. Peter (our first Pope) was so full of the Holy Spirit, that people would be set free from demons and healed just by walking close to him!

✦ Acts 5:16. People brought into Jerusalem the sick and those with unclean spirits and they were all healed!

✦ Acts 8: 4-8. Many healed through Philip's preaching in Samaria.

✦ Acts 9: 32-34. Peter heals a man that was paralyzed for eight years. Two entire cities turned to Jesus because of this!

✦ Acts 9: 36-42. Peter resurrects Dorcas.

✦ Acts 14: 8-10. Paul heals a cripple from birth.

✦ Acts 19: 11-12. People got healed and set free from demons just by touching aprons and handkerchiefs that Paul had touched.

✦ Acts 20: 7-13. Paul raises Eutychus from the dead.

The early church prayed for boldness to preach the Word of God and asked the Lord to back them up with healings, signs and wonders:

Healing is for You!

"...grant to your servants to speak thy Word with all boldness, while thou stretchest out thy hand to heal, and signs and wonders are performed through the name of thy holy servant Jesus." (Acts 4:29-20).

Everywhere that I'm invited to preach, I expect the Lord to heal, because that is His nature; I expect signs and wonders! This is His promise! This brings Him great glory! After all, He's alive! Signs and wonders also cause people to repent and turn to Jesus, because they point to Him (Matthew 11: 20-24). This is part of the Great Commission (Mark 16: 15-18). As a child of God my job is to see that God's kingdom is released "on earth as it is in heaven." Last year in Uganda (2005) as we preached, many people repented and committed their lives to Jesus; in addition, the Lord healed and set many people free. These are just some of the most notable testimonies:

✦ One lady who had many hernias and was scheduled for surgery, was miraculously healed. The hernias disappeared and her stomach became smooth.

✦ Another lady who had to be carried into the meeting because she very sick, was completely healed from all her pains and aches; she left dancing and rejoicing!

✦ One man, the father of a priest, was set free from a depression that had lasted five years. He witnessed to the power of the Holy Spirit the joy he was experiencing!

✦ One lady who for forty years had not been able to sleep because of demonic attacks at night, was delivered and set free; she was able to sleep through the night and was full of joy!

✦ One lady healed of a bleeding problem.

✦ One lady was able to eat and not feel sick for the first time in years.

Healing is Your Inheritance!

✦ One man received a major healing in his feet and came back wearing shoes for the first time in years!

✦ The wife of a prayer group leader was healed of a major back problem; she was able to walk and bend sideways and up and down without pain.

✦ Many that were demonized were set free!

In Gangama parish, several Muslims turned to Jesus when they saw the power of God. They realized that our Jesus is alive! They were baptized that Sunday. Two ex-Catholics also returned to the Church when they saw that the Holy Spirit is alive and well in our Church. Alleluia!

"But seek first His kingdom and His righteousness, and all these things shall be yours as well." (Matthew 6:33).

Healing is for You!

YOUR SICKNESS IS NOT YOUR CROSS!

> "And He said to all, "If any man
> Would come after me, let him deny
> Himself and take up his cross daily
> And follow me." (Luke 9:23).

The cross that the Lord wants us to take up daily is a death to self, a complete denial and renunciation of our self-life and self-will. Ouch! He wants us "dead!" Dead to the works of the flesh; St. Paul says in Romans 6:11,

> "So you must consider yourselves dead to sin and alive to God in Christ Jesus."

This involves living for Him and not for ourselves any longer. It means that it's His will, His plans, His purposes, His desires that take precedence in our lives. "So therefore, whoever of you does not renounce all that he has cannot be my disciple" (Luke 14:33). We are alive in this planet for Him; we do not belong to ourselves any longer because He has bought us and redeemed us from the hand of the devil through His blood (Ephesians 1:7). We are not our own. We put Him and His kingdom first. The Apostle Paul says in 1 Corinthians 6: 19-20 "…You are not your own; you were bought with a price…." Jesus also said:

> "If anyone comes to me and does not hate his own father
> and mother and wife and children and brothers and sisters,
> yes, and even his own life, he cannot be my disciple.
> Whoever does not bear his own cross and come after me,
> cannot be my disciple." (Luke 14:25-27).

As you see, "carrying the cross" is not about a broken toe, cancer or a headache; He wants to heal you of those things! It's about getting out of the way and putting Him first in everything;

a continuous yielding to the Holy Spirit in every situation. An example of the cross could be the mockery, persecution and ridicule that comes to the followers of Jesus because we don't do the things we use to do. "They are surprised that you do not now join them in the same wild profligacy, and they abuse you..." (1 Peter 4:4). Another example of the cross would be getting fired from your job because of your faith, or being disowned by your family because you now follow Jesus. "For whoever is ashamed of Me and of My words, of him will the Son of man be ashamed...." (Luke 9:26). This year in Tanzania I met a former Muslim who now follows Jesus. The authorities in his mosque beat him up and wanted to kill him; his own family disowned him. When I met him he had no money, no food and no place to sleep. This is the cross. "For whoever would save his life will lose it; and whoever loses his life for My sake and the gospel's will save it. For what does it profit a man, to gain the whole world and forfeit his life?" (Mark 8:35-36).

More examples of the cross is the inconvenience (maybe driving a few miles out of your way to pick up a sister who doesn't drive) or discomfort (sleeping in a hot room in the mission field when you're used to a nice, cool temperature at home). My friend and brother, Fred Mawanda, from Masaka, Uganda, owns a van which he uses to transport believers back and forth every time there is a meeting or a conference. Out of ten thousands Catholic charismatics in his city, there are only two vehicles! He spends hours driving God's people back and forth from the meetings. Why does he do that? He knows that the Lord blessed him with a van not just for himself and his family, but also to help extend God's kingdom. He's committed to transporting God's people as needed. I imagine that at times he would rather be doing something else! Considering that the early Christians were thrown to the lions because of their faith, our "crosses" in America are small compared to theirs. However, the 20th century saw many martyred for the sake of Christ in many third world countries.

Healing is for You!

The revelation of Jesus from the Scriptures shows that He healed the sick, not that He made people sick. So many times I hear believers say "God sent me this disease...." If you think that your sickness is your cross and that God sent you that disease, I suggest that you quit going to the doctors in order to get healed. The cross is something that we willingly embrace, not something that we try to get rid of. So if you're trying to get rid of your sickness, which you think is your cross, then you're being disobedient in trying to get rid of it. Why pay medical insurance if you think that your sickness is your cross?

"Others suffered mocking and scourging, and even chains and imprisonment. They were stoned, they were sawn in two, they were killed with the sword; they went about in skins of sheep and goats, destitute, afflicted, ill-treated...." (Hebrews 11:36-37)

Healing is Your Inheritance!

HEALING: A BLESSING OF THE KINGDOM!

"Pray then like this:
> Our Father who art in heaven,
> Hallowed be thy name.
> Thy kingdom come,
> Thy will be done,
> On earth as it is in heaven."
> (Matthew 6:9-10).

Jesus came to establish God's kingdom here on earth and He taught His disciples to pray to the Father that His kingdom would be established "on earth as it is in heaven." In other words, we are to bring "heaven" down into any troubled situation or person on planet earth. We as God's people are to release the blessings of the kingdom; healing is one of those blessings of the kingdom of God. Is there sickness and disease in heaven? No! Mental illness, depression, despair, arthritis, cancer, headaches, anxiety attacks, miscarriages, addictions in heaven? Of course not! Then we can release "heaven" into any person needing healing! This is the Lord's will; to bring the blessing of healing where it's needed.

In two of His parables Jesus made it clear how we are to respond to the sick and hurting: we are to show mercy and compassion and release healing. In the parable of the Good Samaritan (Luke 10: 30-37), it was not the priest or Levite that pleased God, but the "uneducated and ignorant" Samaritan that showed compassion to the man that was beat up, stripped and half-dead. It was the Samaritan that stopped and "bound up his wounds;" the priest and Levite walked away from the hurting man. In the parable of The Rich Man and Lazarus (Luke 16: 19-31), the rich man's attitude towards Lazarus revealed the hardened condition of his heart: no compassion for the sick and hurting. The rich man, even though he had "everything" in his power to help Lazarus, showed no mercy to him, a poor man at his gate. Lazarus had so many sores that "the dogs came and licked his sores" (v.

21). Even the dogs responded in a more godly way to Lazarus' sores than the rich man! I know many people today that prefer animals to human beings; do you wonder why?

If you are a child of God, the blessings of the kingdom are your inheritance; healing is your inheritance! Healing is ours to receive and to release! "You received without pay, give without pay." (Matthew 10: 7b). The fact is that He has already provided for your healing. 1 Peter 2:24 says:

"By His wounds you have been healed."

Another fact is that we have been empowered by the Holy Spirit with gifts of healing to fulfill the mandate to heal the sick, just like Jesus! Jesus said in John 14:12

"Truly, truly, I say to you, he who believes in Me will also do the works that I do; and greater works than these will he do, because I go to the Father." Healing is one of those "works!" James says "faith apart from works is dead" (James 2: 26). Let's wake up, church! Let's rise up and carry on with His works! Everywhere that Jesus went He released the blessings of the kingdom; He healed, delivered, set people free. Jesus Himself was the kingdom of God while He was here on earth. He disrupted every funeral He attended by raising the person from the dead! Matthew says in chapter 4: 23-24

"And He went about all Galilee, teaching in their synagogues and preaching the gospel of the kingdom and healing every disease and every infirmity among the people. So His fame spread throughout all Syria, and they brought Him all the sick, those afflicted with various diseases and pains, demoniacs, epileptics, and paralytics, and he healed them."

Again, Matthew writes:

Healing is Your Inheritance!

"And Jesus went about all the cities and villages, teaching in their synagogues and preaching the gospel of the kingdom, and healing every disease and every infirmity." (Matthew 9: 35).

Matthew makes the point that Jesus went about teaching, preaching and healing. He "went about" doing this. This was His ministry. He taught the people about the kingdom of God and put what He taught and preached into action. His fame spread so much that "great crowds came to Him, bringing with them the lame, the maimed, the blind, the dumb, and many others, and they put them at His feet, and he healed them, so that the throng wondered, when they saw the dumb speaking, the maimed whole, the lame walking, and the blind seeing; they glorified the God of Israel." (Matthew 15:28-31

We are comfortable with the teaching and preaching ministries of Jesus; but why ignore the healing ministry of Jesus, when it was so dear to His heart and He clearly commanded His followers to do the same? Why on earth did He give us "gifts of healing for?" He said that we would do even "greater works!" (John 14:12). The healing ministry of Jesus reveals His love and compassion for the sick and hurting; as we grow in Him, His love and compassion grows in us. As we are transformed to look like Jesus, we should expect to grow in His love and compassion for those afflicted with sickness and disease. There should be something inside of us that wants to make wrong things right. Lord, break our hearts for the sick and suffering!

The kingdom of God is within us (Luke 17: 21) (NKJ); as we go we can bring healing to those that are suffering! Let me give you an example of what I mean. My friend Ina's manicurist had tremendous pain in her shoulder; she could hardly do her job. (As a single mother, that's how she earns her living. If she can't work, she will not have any money to support herself and her child.) Ina laid her hand on her shoulder and released the healing of the kingdom. (We don't have to be in church to pray!) As the day progressed, her shoulder got completely healed and pain free. The manicurist could not stop thanking the Lord throughout the day and proclaimed it everywhere she went, giving glory to Jesus! Alleluia!

In Dar Es Salaam, Tanzania we were asked to go to the hospital and pray for a relative of a charismatic leader. We not only prayed for this person, but we also prayed for ten more people in that ward. We saw two miraculous healings out of the eleven; others progressively started to improve. One old Anglican man in his eighties was hospitalized because for two weeks he had not been able to walk; we laid our hands on his legs and in the name of Jesus released the healing of the kingdom. I told him "Try walking; I will hold you as you try." The man got up and started walking as he held on to me. Then he said to me, "Don't hold me." He started to walk on his own and made it back and forth to his bed. Can you imagine how happy he was? He thanked the Lord for His mercy and compassion. Alleluia! Another young man, a Lutheran, was under great respiratory distress with an asthma attack; he could hardly breathe. We prayed and very soon he could breathe normally again. Thank you, Jesus!

After Jesus healed the leper, Luke writes in Chapter 5:15 "But so much the more the report went abroad concerning Him; and great multitudes gathered to hear and be healed or their infirmities." Again in Chapter 6: 17-19, Luke makes the point that people came "to hear Him and to be healed of their diseases; and those who were troubled with unclean spirits were cured. And all the crowd sought to touch Him, for power came forth from Him and healed them all."

I can't wait for the day when ambulances transporting sick people would first ask this question: Where is the nearest Catholic Church?

Healing is Your Inheritance!

A LONG LIFE: A BLESSING OF THE KINGDOM

"With long life I will satisfy him, and show him my salvation." (Psalm 91:16).

Long life is a blessing from the Lord. As we walk with the Lord and "abide in the shadow of the Almighty" (Psalm 91: 1), we can expect a long, fruitful life. Abiding in Him and being led by the Holy Spirit will enable us to experience "the goodness of the Lord in the land of the living" (Psalm 27: 13). There are many promises of long life in the Bible connected with walking in obedience to the Lord. The command to honor father and mother comes accompanied with the promise of a long life (Deuteronomy 5:16):

> "Honor your father and your mother, as the Lord your God commanded you; that your days may be prolonged and that it may go well with you, in the land which the Lord your God gives you."

In the New Testament, in Ephesians 6: 2-3, the Apostle Paul reminds us of this commandment and the promise that comes with obeying it:

> "Honor your father and mother" (this is the first commandment with a promise), "that it may be well with you and that you may live long on the earth."

Proverbs 9:10-11 clearly shows that as we walk in the fear of the Lord we are blessed with a long life:

> "The fear of the Lord is the beginning of wisdom,
> And the knowledge of the Holy One is insight.
> For by Me your days will be multiplied,
> And years will be added to your life."

Father Abraham, the father of our faith, was blessed with
a long, fruitful life. He was blessed in every way! Think of
it; he was blessed in EVERY way. This means that Abraham
was blessed with health, long life, healing, abundance, victory,
relationships. Genesis 24:1 says:

"Now Abraham was old, well advanced in years; and
the Lord had blessed Abraham in all things." Because
Abraham is the father of our faith, what the Lord did for
him can be ours too. As we walk by faith, like Abraham
walked, following the Lord in every way, we can expect the
same blessings, a long life included!

Proverbs 3:1-2 says,

"My son, do not forget my teaching, but let your heart keep
my commandments; For length of days and years of life
and abundant welfare will they give you."

We see again that walking in obedience to God's Word brings
great blessings to us, including a long life. When we disobey, we
leave the boundaries of His protection and covering. For example,
the Bible clearly reveals that sexual immorality is sin and not
pleasing to the Lord. When we are sexually promiscuous, we
expose ourselves to many different types of sexually transmitted
diseases and we could get sick. God is not to blame; we are the
ones responsible. I ministered to AIDS patients for many years; so
many blamed God for the virus, even when they had a long history
of sexual immorality! His boundaries are very clear in His Word
and there is great protection in keeping His commandments. "The
fear of the Lord prolongs life…" (Proverbs 10:27).

Finding God's wisdom and allowing it to guide our lives will
make a difference:

"Long life is in her right hand; in her left hand are riches and honor. Her ways are ways of pleasantness, and all her paths are peace. She is a tree of life to those who lay hold of her; those who hold her fast are called happy."

Even the way we use our tongue affects our longevity:

"Come, O sons, listen to Me, I will teach you the fear of the Lord. What man is there who desires life, and covets many days, that He may enjoy good? Keep your tongue from evil, and your Lips from speaking deceit. Depart from evil, and do good; Seek peace and pursue it." (Psalm 34: 11-14).

"The years of our life are threescore and ten (70 years), or even by reason of strength fourscore (80 years)...." (Psalm 90:10).

CONTEND FOR YOUR INHERITANCE

"Beloved, being very eager to write to you of our common salvation, I found it necessary to write appealing to you to contend for the faith. Which was once for all delivered to the saints." (Titus 3).

We are not to be passive about the benefits of our salvation, but rather be spiritually aggressive. Remember that there are "giants in the land" (Numbers 13: 31-33), enemies and mindsets that keep us from what rightly belongs to us as children of God. Imagine for a moment that your grandfather passed away and left you and your family an awesome inheritance worth a lot of money. However, someone pretending to be you, an impostor and liar, is trying to get your inheritance. Would you allow him to do such a thing, or would you fight him? It's the same thing with the spiritual blessings that Jesus won for us in Calvary! Don't allow the enemy to keep you fooled and deceived with his lies! Don't let him stop you from appropriating what is rightfully yours! Healing is part of your land! Jesus Himself said in Matthew 11:12

"...the kingdom of heaven suffers violence, and the violent take it by force." (NKJ).

If the only thing that Jesus wanted when He died on the Cross for us was to take us to heaven one day, then we would already be there. That fact that we're still here means that we're here on earth for a purpose. There is a plan and purpose for each one of us. As children of God, redeemed by His blood and filled with His Holy Spirit, we're supposed to be extending His kingdom here "on earth as it is in heaven" and bringing in the great harvest of unbelievers into His kingdom; we're supposed to be carrying on with "his works" (John 14:12). As I write there are over 4 billion people that still need to come to Christ. What does healing have to do with evangelization? A lot! It's central to the preaching of the Gospel;

it points to Jesus and shows that Jesus is alive! He is glorified! it's His command! it shows the love, compassion and power of Jesus! In addition, to carry on with the works of Jesus we need to be strong and healthy!

Many people don't live a long, fruitful life because the enemy comes to "steal, kill and destroy" (John 10:10) their lives and they don't defend themselves. They are just very passive with the doctor's report. They might have faith in Jesus for salvation and forgiveness of sins, but no faith in Jesus for healing. Peter says:

"Be sober, be watchful. Your adversary the devil prowls around like a roaring lion seeking some one to devour. Resist him, firm in your faith...." (1 Peter 5: 8-9).

We are not to be afraid of the devil; he's a defeated foe (Colossians 2:15). However, we do need to be vigilant and aware that he wants to destroy us. He can attack us in different ways so that our days on earth are cut short: sickness and disease; car accidents; drug addiction and alcoholism; suicide; wars; famine and hunger; abortion; curses; death. All of this is meant to destroy our lives so that we are rendered useless, paralyzed, ineffective and neutralized for Kingdom purposes. Many of us remain passive to the enemy's attacks on our health and believe every negative report as the last word because of ignorance of God's Word. "My people are destroyed for lack of knowledge...." (Hosea 4:6). However, we don't have to accept and resign ourselves to the enemy's plan for our lives; we don't have to believe his lies. We are to rise up in the power of the Holy Spirit and take authority over him in the name of Jesus. Luke 10:19 says,

"Behold, I have given you authority to tread upon serpents and scorpions, and over all the power of the enemy; and nothing shall hurt you."

Include sickness and disease in the category of "serpents and scorpions!" Stop calling it "my" disease and start treading on it! It isn't yours; Dr. Jesus already carried it on the Cross! Our enemies were defeated in the Cross (Colossians 2:15) and now is up to us to enforce the victory that Jesus won for us. 1 John 4:4 says that "…He who is in you is greater that he who is in the world." As temples of the Holy Spirit, let's tell sickness and disease that they're not welcome into our bodies and start rebuking them in the name of Jesus! Look at what Jesus did when Peter's mother-in-law was sick with a fever:

> "And He stood over her and rebuked the fever, and it left her; and immediately she rose and served them." (Luke 4:39).

One morning I woke up dizzy; the ceiling seemed to be spinning and I had no balance. I was supposed to give a talk at the prayer group that morning. The night before I had gone to bed completely healthy and I could not understand what had happened. I said, "I will go to the prayer group and give the talk even if I have to crawl." I discerned that this was an attack from the enemy and proceeded to lay hands on my head and prayed in tongues. As I prayed in tongues and put holy water on my head, "something" lifted off and I was immediately set free. Thank you, Jesus! Imagine, if I had not had discernment, I would have crawled back into bed and cancelled the talk. That's exactly what the enemy wanted!

> "Behold, I have set the land before you; go in and take possession of the land…." (Deut. 1:8).

Healing is Your Inheritance!

HOLY SPIRIT: AGENT OF HEALING

"If the Spirit of Him who raised Jesus from the dead dwells in you, He who raised Christ Jesus from the dead will give life to your mortal Bodies also through His Spirit who dwells in you." (Romans 8:11).

The same Spirit that raised Jesus from the dead dwells inside of us! Is He capable of bringing healing and life into our bodies? Of course! He raised Jesus from the dead, didn't He? He can certainly heal us of anything in our souls and bodies that needs healing. There is resurrection power inside of us releasing life to our bodies. It's through the workings of the Holy Spirit that we receive God's benefits, including His healing. The Holy Spirit comes loaded with gifts, including gifts of healing, which is one of the nine manifestations of the Holy Spirit. When the Holy Spirit is released in your life, expect healing to be released!

Jesus refers to the Holy Spirit as "rivers of living water" (John 7: 38-39). Imagine not just one river, but "rivers" of living water flowing out from our innermost being releasing healing, refreshing and restoration. The helper, the Holy Spirit, releases the help that we need spiritually, emotionally, physically. Our challenge is to keep the "rivers" constantly flowing from "the wells of salvation" (Isaiah 12:3) inside us. Make sure your wells are not clogged with "debris" of unforgiveness, anger, resentment, bitterness, hatred, fear, sin, discouragement! These will hinder the "flow" of the Spirit in your life.

There is also a river of life in the throne of God; is this a coincidence, or is the Lord trying to show us something? John writes:

"Then He showed me the river of the water of life, bright as crystal, flowing from the throne of God and of the Lamb through the middle of the street of the city; also on either side of the river, the tree of life with its twelve kinds

Of fruit, yielding its fruit each month; and the leaves of the tree were for the healing of the nations." (Revelation 22:1-2).

Picture yourself as "the city" with the river of life flowing within you. "There is a river whose streams make glad the city of God...." (Psalm 46:4). This river releases life, joy and healing. It's the water from the river that produces healing in the leaves of the tree. This is the Holy Spirit!

In the beautiful passage of Ezekiel 48, where the prophet has an awesome experience with the "water" flowing in the Temple, he writes:

"And wherever the River goes every living creature which swarms will live, and there will be very many fish; for this water goes there, that the waters of the sea may become fresh; so everything will live where the river goes." (v.9). Continuing in verse 12

"And on the banks, on both sides of the river, there will grow all kinds of trees for food. Their leaves will not wither or their fruit fail, but they will bear fresh fruit every month, because the water for them flows from the sanctuary. Their fruit will be for food and their leaves for healing."

Notice once again the connection between the river and the leaves of the trees producing healing. It's very clear that the Holy Spirit, the river of life, releases life, healing and restoration! Any dry, parched, barren, sterile or thirsty land in your life? Let the Holy Spirit touch you. Let Him heal you and change you into an instrument of life and healing in this world. Appreciate the Holy Spirit inside of you; He is your helper. Live your life knowing that He is there for you in every way; create an atmosphere in your life where He is wanted, appreciated and welcomed! Learn to yield

Healing is Your Inheritance!

to Him at all times and experience His healing! Not only does He want to heal you, but He wants to use you to heal others!

> "...but whoever drinks of the water that I shall give Him will never thirst; the water that I shall give him Will become in him a spring of living water welling Up to eternal life." (John 4: 14).

Healing is for You!

II

How to Access Your Healing

Jesus is the healer, but there are different ways in which we can receive His healing. Even if your healing comes through medicine, it is Jesus healing you. It's important that we get to know Him as our healer, especially in these troubled times that we live in with the threat of terrorism, new diseases and biological warfare. Certain diseases have even become resistant to medicine! Start believing and exercising faith for small healings, like head aches or sore throats, and in this way your faith will be built up to believe Him for more healings. Faith is like a muscle that needs to be exercised. Lay hands on your children and release the healing of the kingdom! The Lord not only wants to heal you; He wants to use you as His instrument to bring salvation, healing and deliverance to a sick and dying world. We are called to walk in the same way as He walked (1 John 2:6). As we bring healing to others, we are really reflecting the goodness and kindness of the Lord. Often, this will lead people to repent and turn to Jesus. As the Apostle Paul says in Romans 2:4 "Do you not know that God's kindness is meant to lead you to repentance?"

Healing is for You!

HEALING IN PRAYER AND THE LAYING ON OF HANDS

"Is any one among you sick? Let him call for the elders of
the church, and let them pray over him, anointing him with
oil in the name of the Lord; And the prayer of faith will
save the sick man, and the Lord will raise him up;
And if he has committed sins, he will be forgiven." (James
5:14-15).

This is the instruction for what a believer should do when he
becomes sick: "call for the elders of the church." Many times
the sick person doesn't call anyone and is upset that nobody has
called him. The Scriptures clearly places the responsibility on the
sick person to take the first step in communicating his problem
to the elders. The "elders" will come and anoint him and will
pray for healing. In the Catholic Church we have the Sacrament
of the Anointing of the Sick. Many people wait until the person
is dying to have him anointed; in reality this should be done right
away because there is healing in this Sacrament! Turn to the Lord
immediately when sickness is diagnosed in your body; don't wait
until the last minute to do so, as many people do.

It is the "prayer of faith" that will save the sick man, not the
"prayer of doubt." In other words, the person who prays does
so believing and standing on the truth of the Word of God: that
on the Cross Jesus carried every sickness and disease and by His
stripes we are healed. The "prayer of faith" doesn't tell God "if
it's Your will" when praying for healing. We know how God
thinks about healing; He has already told us in His Word: "Heal
the Sick" (Matthew 10:8). It's a matter of releasing the healing
of the Kingdom of God. Look at Jesus when He healed the sick:
He never begged the Father; many times He just commanded it!
Here are some examples of how Jesus exercised his authority over
sickness and disease:

30

✦ in Matthew 8: 3, Jesus touched the leper and just told him "…be clean."

✦ in Matthew 9:6, Jesus told the paralytic "Rise, take up your bed and go home."

✦ in Mark 3:5, Jesus told the man with the withered hand "Stretch out your hand."

✦ in Mark 7:34, Jesus told the deaf and dumb man "Ephphatha," that is, "Be opened."

✦ in Luke 7:14, Jesus spoke to a dead man: "Young man, I say to you, arise."

✦ in Luke 13:12, Jesus told a woman that had been bent over for eighteen years, "Woman, you are freed from your infirmity."

✦ in John 5:8, Jesus told a man who had been ill for thirty-eight years, "Rise, take your pallet, and walk."

✦ in John 11:43, Jesus commanded Lazarus (who was dead) to come out of the cave; "Lazarus, come out."

I believe the Lord is raising up a people, that just like Jesus, will exercise their God-given authority over sickness and disease! Will you rise up to the challenge? Don't let fear keep you as a "pew" potato! Rise up in the power of His Spirit, "for God did not give us a spirit of timidity but a spirit of power and love and self-control." (1 Timothy 1:7). Let's bring down those strongholds that keep us thinking that healing was only for the early days of the Church or at best that only a few can really bring healing to others! The command of Jesus to believers, still today, is to heal the sick! (Mark 16: 18). He hasn't changed His agenda. You can pray with

people for healing any where you go, even at the gym! My sister
Fifi has prayed with several young ladies in the gym who couldn't
get pregnant; all of them have conceived and given birth! Alleluia!
It is my experience that most people don't really understand
what Jesus has done for them on the Cross. It's good to explain to
them what the Scriptures say about healing so that faith is released
in them as well.
James says that the sick person should confess his sins so that
he can receive forgiveness:

"Therefore confess your sins to one another, and pray
for one another, that you may be healed. The prayer of a
righteous man has great power in its effects" (James 5: 16).

Confession of sins is connected to physical and inner healing.
Honesty at this point is quite necessary because I have found out
that most people need to forgive those that have harmed them. As
long as there is unforgiveness or unconfessed sin, the enemy has
access to "steal, kill and destroy" (John 10:10) in that person's life.
For us Catholics, participating in the Sacrament of Reconciliation
is a source of inner and physical healing.
One of the things about the Charismatic Renewal that really
touched my heart was to see healing prayer for sick people.
Coming from a family of doctors, I had never seen anyone laying
hands on the sick for healing. Frankly, I didn't know such a
thing existed! During a Life in the Spirit Seminar, it was very
well explained that the Holy Spirit gives us gifts of healing, and
those gifts are for today. After being baptized in the Holy Spirit,
I immediately started laying hands on my children when they got
sick, and my children would get healed. My friend Ina and I would
pray for just anybody that was sick. I remember our first "case"
in the hospital: a young boy in a coma. The doctors didn't know
what else to do and the parents were desperate. Someone asked us
to go and pray. We had only met Jesus a few months ago, but off
we went, full of joy and expectant faith! We prayed and laid hands

on the boy and left. We just knew that the boy was going to wake up, and he did! Alleluia! We were so excited and thankful to the Lord for having used us! But this is His command:

"...You shall lay hands on the sick and they shall recover" (Mark 16: 18).

I have not stopped praying with the sick for healing, even if not everyone gets healed; some have actually died. However, many people stop praying because of lack of results. But we must contend for this benefit of His kingdom! I personally am determined to carry on with this aspect of Jesus' ministry; this is what He wants! He is the healer; we are just His instruments. Today I am seeing more and more people get healed by Jesus. We cannot allow what we see with our eyes water down the Word of God. We must be obedient to His command to heal, even the raising of the dead! Recently in the city of Chicago we prayed and laid hands on a man suffering from a rare type of cancer in his blood; the doctors had told him that he didn't have much longer to live. We explained to him how Jesus had carried every sickness and disease on the Cross. He forgave the people that had hurt him. He repented and committed his life to Jesus. We laid our hands on him for healing. He went back to the doctor for more tests, and the results came back negative. They called long distance to give me the good news. Thank you, Jesus! You still heal today!

My brother prayed and laid hands on a 60-year-old patient; a lady with a frozen back with pain and inability to bend over. She had suffered like this for 20 years. After prayer she could bend over and move without pain! Not only that, she got filled with the Holy Spirit and began to speak in tongues. She was full of joy. She told my brother she was a Jehovah Witness, but decided to give her life to Jesus, the One who had healed her! This lady not only received physical healing, but the gift of salvation in Christ Jesus. The Holy Spirit used the healing to reveal and point to Jesus as Lord and Savior! Amen.

Healing is for You!

"So they remained for a long time, speaking boldly for the Lord, who bore witness to the word of His grace, granting signs and wonders to be done by their hands." (Acts 14:3).

How to Access Your Healing

HEALING IN THE WORD OF GOD

"My son, be attentive to My words;
Incline your ear to my saying.
Let them not escape from your sight;
Keep them within your heart.
For they are life to him who finds them,
And healing to their flesh." (Proverbs 4:22).

There is healing in the Word of God. According to this passage, the Scriptures bring life and healing into our bodies as we become "doers of the Word" (James 1:22). This is really good news! Something happens to us when we regularly spend time in the Scriptures. Not only are our minds renewed, but our physical bodies receive healing from "eating" the bread of the Word. There are healing benefits in the Word of God. This "medicine" you can take as often as you want! I have personally experienced better health myself since I surrendered my life to Jesus and feed on His Word daily. I used to get bad colds with fever and sore throats regularly; today I hardly get them. Thank you, Jesus! I attribute this fact to being in His Word. But the Lord wants to do more than just heal us superficially, since we are spirit, soul and body (1 Thessalonians 5: 23). His Word is:

"sharper than any two-edged sword, piercing to the division of soul and spirit, of joints and marrow, and discerning the thoughts and intentions of the heart" (Hebrews 4: 12).

Since the human heart is "deceitful above all things, and desperately corrupt" (Jeremiah 17: 9), we really need the "scalpel" of the Word to go deep within us to reveal and deal with deep-rooted sin and iniquity in our lives. For example, a "root of bitterness" (Hebrews 12: 15) causes trouble and "many become defiled." Bitterness is like poison, not only affecting the person spiritually, emotionally and physically, but her relationships as well. As we allow the Holy Spirit to use the healing instrument of God's Word to reveal and deal with evil roots in our hearts, and we respond by repenting and renouncing them, our bodies will experience more healing and health. Those open doors to the enemy will be closed and he can no longer come to "steal, kill and destroy" (John 10:10). In addition, hurts, pains and festering inner wounds that we have not dealt with will start getting healed as we allow God's word to penetrate deep within. It was only when I came to Jesus that my eyes were opened and I realized that I was carrying pain from rejection from certain incidents in my childhood. As I forgave those relatives and blessed them, a great healing and peace started to take place deep within. Thank you, Jesus!

In Matthew 8:8 the centurion who came to Jesus asking for healing for his servant told Him,

"Lord, I'm not worthy to have you come under my roof; but just say the Word and my servant shall be healed." (This is what we say before receiving Holy Communion; do we really believe what we're proclaiming?).

The centurion understood that the words of Jesus contained the power in themselves to accomplish and carry out what they were supposed to do. He also understood that His words were not limited by time or space. Isaiah 55:11 says,

"...so shall My Word be that goes forth from my mouth; It shall not return to me empty, but it shall accomplish That which I purpose, and prosper in the thing for which I sent it."

The Lord told the prophet Jeremiah:

"...for I am watching over my Word to perform it." (Jeremiah 1:12).

The Lord Himself makes sure that His Word is fulfilled! The prophet Joel says:

"...He that executes His Word is powerful" (Joel 2:11). The Lord carries out what His Word is meant to do, because He is not a liar (Numbers 23:19).

Jesus Himself said that His Word is like a "seed" (Mark 4). When a seed is planted in good soil it produces what it is meant to produce. For example, an apple seed will eventually become an apple tree bearing apples. The Word of God, which is a "seed" containing healing, will start releasing what it contains: healing. When Jesus becomes the most precious person in our lives, His Word becomes a treasure in our hearts. "Pleasant words are like a honeycomb, sweetness to the soul and health to the body." (Proverbs 16:24). We are attentive to His Words, we develop a listening ear, we hold on to the promises; we obey His Word and we receive His healing benefits as we do so. Proverbs 3: 7-8 says:

"Be not wise in your own eyes; fear the Lord, and turn away from evil. It will be healing to your flesh and refreshment to your bones."

Abiding in Him and coming under His lordship will affect our bodies. Living in obedience to the Lord and submitting to His Word releases healing and refreshment. Instead of being anxious, we trust; instead of holding grudges, bitterness and resentment, we forgive; instead of cursing, we bless; instead of being proud, we humble ourselves; instead of trying to control we let God control. "Anxiety in a man's heart weighs him down, but a good word makes him glad." (Proverbs 12:25). The result of aligning our lives to His Word is that a great peace comes into our lives as we trust God, which is beneficial to our health. "Great peace have those who love Thy law..." (Psalm 119: 165). Isaiah 26:3 says,

Healing is for You!

"Thou dost keep him in perfect peace,
Whose mind is stayed on Thee,
Because he trusts in Thee."

Perfect peace! What a way to live! Only Jesus, the Prince of
Peace can give it to you! It doesn't come from drugs or alcohol,
your bank account, or circumstances! The word used here for
peace is "shalom," which means much more than what we think:
completeness, wholeness, peace, health, welfare, safety, soundness,
tranquility, prosperity, perfectness, fullness, rest, harmony; the
absence of agitation or discord. It means the total and complete
welfare of the person, in spirit, soul and body. You can't beat that!
There is also great joy in God's word; and this joy of the Lord
is our strength! (Nehemiah 8:10). How we need new strength
daily to face each day in victory and not with an attitude of defeat!
An attitude of defeat and negativity brings our physical defenses
down; joy actually boosts our immune system!

"I rejoice at Thy Word like one who finds great spoil."
(Psalm 119: 162).

"Thy words were found, and I ate them, and Thy words
became to me a joy and the delight of my heart…."
(Jeremiah 15: 16).

To live in peace and joy is our inheritance, "For the kingdom
of God does not mean food and drink but righteousness and peace
and joy in the Holy Spirit…" (Romans 14: 17). Anything less
(anxiety, fear, depression, panic) is not what God has destined for
us. How many people do you know that live in peace and joy?

"He sent forth His Word, and healed them, and delivered
them from destruction" (Psalm 107: 20).

HEALING IN HIS MANIFEST PRESENCE

"Yet Thou are holy, enthroned in the praises of Israel."
(Psalm 22:3).

God is omnipresent, however His manifest presence is not
everywhere. There is an atmosphere where the Lord inhabits and
makes His presence felt: the atmosphere of praise and worship,
which is the atmosphere of heaven. When we praise and worship
Him in "spirit and in truth" expect a mighty move of the Holy
Spirit. In the manifest presence of the Lord, great things happen
because we are releasing the atmosphere of the kingdom through
our praises. The Holy Spirit starts doing the same things that King
Jesus would do if He was physically present: people get healed and
delivered; people experience freedom, joy and refreshing. Psalm
147: 1-3 gives a description of the ministry of Jesus:

"Praise the Lord! For it is good to sing praises to our God;
for He is gracious, and a song of praise is seemly. The
Lord builds up Jerusalem; He gathers the outcasts of Israel.
He heals the brokenhearted, and binds up their wounds."
There, in an atmosphere of praise He still builds up,
gathers, heals and binds our wounds by His Spirit!

Psalm 87: 2 says

"...the Lord loves the gates of Zion more than all the
dwelling places of Jacob."

What are the gates of Zion? The gates of praise!! There in
Mount Zion King David placed the ark of His presence under a
tent, and there was 24-hour praise and worship directed to the
King of all Kings! As a matter of fact, in these days this is what
the Lord is wanting to restore (Acts 15: 15-18). Could one of the
reasons be that He wants His people healed and restored? In the

nation of Zambia, in Mongu province, we held a service in one of the out-stations. There was a mat placed for the "very sick" near the altar; there were eleven of them. Some had to be carried in because they were too sick to walk. As we were praising the Lord, I noticed that two of the very sick had gotten up by themselves and were dancing; eventually five more got up to dance! Their faces were transformed and radiant in the presence of the Lord. Obviously, they had received some sort of healing for them to get up and dance! The Holy Spirit Himself started to minister to them in the midst of the praises! Alleluia!

In our prayer group there has been many healings and deliverances just from being in the presence of the Lord: broken bones have been healed, growth in the breasts and ovaries dissolved, freedom from depression, confusion and negativity are some of the ways in which the Lord has healed His people. Lately the Lord has been healing teeth in many of the ladies that attend our group. Even their dentists have commented that their teeth and gums look much better! Last month in Tanzania many people got freed from depression, insomnia, headaches, teeth problems, digestion and intestinal problems, pains and aches, just from being in the presence of the Lord! Alleluia!

"Let God arise, let His enemies be scattered…." (Psalm 68:1).

When Jesus is exalted and lifted up, His enemies flee! Sickness and disease are enemies; depression, despair, anxiety, fear, panic attacks are enemies; they have to flee! At the name of Jesus, the name above all other names, every knee has to bow! The enemy can't stand the presence of the Lord when Jesus is enthroned in our praises. He was kicked out of heaven because his pride did not allow him to submit to Jesus. We displace him when we bow before Jesus and worship Him right here on planet earth! Psalm 149 is very clear about the "high" praises of God in our mouths: our praises become a weapon that binds the enemy and drives him out:

"Let the high praises of God be in their throats and two-edged swords in their hands; To wreak vengeance on the nations and chastisement on the peoples, to bind their kings with chains and their nobles with fetters of iron..." (Psalm 149:6-8).

Every Saturday when we go to the women's jail we praise and worship the Lord before the preaching of the Word. Many healings take place during this time; especially with depressed inmates. Many are set free and filled with joy; headaches, back pains, digestive problems, knee pains, gone as we worship the Lord! On Saturday morning many inmates can't wait to come to the service, because they know they will be changed and healed by the Spirit of God. One inmate got healed from ulcers through a word of knowledge; she said "I didn't know that Jesus heals today!" This healing totally changed her life around as she experienced the love of Jesus for herself personally. After being released from jail, she found a church, went back to school and started helping in the church with the children in Sunday school. Her transformation and restoration started with a physical healing. Thank you, Jesus!

Another great benefit of being in the manifest presence of the Lord is His joy:

"...in Thy presence there is fullness of joy...." (Psalm 16:11).

What does joy have to do with health? "The joy of the Lord is my strength!" (Nehemiah 8:10). We have strength to overcome whatever comes against me! It is medically known that when a person is depressed or anxious, her defenses are down, and it is easier for the body to give in to sickness. The joy of the Lord becomes like a wall of protection against our enemies! Spending time in the manifest presence of the Lord is beneficial to our health!

"Let everything that breathes praise the Lord." (Psalm 150:6).

Healing is for You!

HEALING IN THE GIFTS OF THE HOLY SPIRIT

"Now there are varieties of gifts, but the same Spirit; and there are varieties of service, but the same Lord; and there are varieties of working; but it is the same God who inspires them all in every one. To each is given the manifestation of the Spirit for the common good." (1 Corinthians 12: 4-7).

As you see, these gifts are given to us for the "common good." They are given to us so that we too can release the love, compassion and power of Jesus to others. There are nine gifts or manifestations of the Holy Spirit (1 Corinthians 12:8-10):

> "To one is given through the Spirit the utterance of wisdom, and to another the utterance of knowledge according to the same Spirit, to another faith, by the same Spirit, to another gifts of healing by the one Spirit, to another the working of miracles, to another prophecy, to another the ability to distinguish between spirits, to another various kinds of tongues, to another the interpretation of tongues."

The Holy Spirit is the gift, and He comes loaded with these gifts so that we can carry on with the works of Jesus (John 14:12). The public ministry of Jesus was a charismatic ministry, because these gifts were in operation as He ministered to the people. Remember, Jesus lived down here as man and He received the empowerment of the Holy Spirit at the River Jordan. (Matthew 3:16; Mark 1:10; Luke 3:22; John 1:32). There are "gifts of healing," (not just one gift), because there are many different kinds of sicknesses and diseases. The Lord has wonderfully equipped us so that we too can "destroy the works of the devil" (1 John 3:8) and "walk in the same way in which He walked" (1 John 2:6). If we want to be effective in ministry and see people healed and made whole, we need the Holy Spirit! We can't do it on our own! I personally call the gifts of the Holy Spirit "love in action," because they empower us to love people powerfully. In other words, we can do something more in a difficult situation than just sympathize, empathize, and hold the sick person's hand (even though these are important); we can actually release the healing of the kingdom through the healing gifts of the Holy Spirit! This is a wonderful way of keeping the second greatest commandment: "You shall love your neighbor as yourself." (Matthew 22:39). Because we love the person, we can actually make an awesome difference in that person's life. St. Paul says that what matters is "faith working through love." (Galatians 5:6). Love is the motivation for the use of the gifts; the love of Jesus inside us and love for others. I remember one time when my mother was very sick with an intestinal problem and was just dreading to go to the hospital. As a good daughter, I was ready to take her to the hospital, stay with her and hold her hand. However, King Jesus directed me to lay hands on her stomach and pray for healing. My sister and I prayed in tongues, laid our hands in her stomach, and the healing started to flow into her body. Within an hour she was back to normal. Alleluia! My mother was so happy that she didn't have to be hospitalized! She praised the Lord for His love and faithfulness for her!

The "gifts of healing" are for healing of the sick; not just for the physical body, but also for spiritual, mental and emotional healing. The Lord wants to heal us inside out! He wants to go deep and heal the inner wounds and hurts that keep us down, which in turn affect our physical bodies as well. The gift of "word of knowledge" works very powerfully together with the gifts of healing. The gift of the word of knowledge is revelation from the Holy Spirit; for example, it could be revelation of the root cause of a sickness as you are praying with an individual, or a "word" of what the Holy Spirit is healing at that moment in a group of people. I just came back from a big conference and the Lord gave me many "words of knowledge," including healing of the gums and teeth. One lady that had gone to the conference with an abcess in her gums was healed instantly as she appropriated that "word"

for herself. The abcess disappeared! In Tanzania, there were tons
of healings that took place through the "word of knowledge,"
including healings of bleeding from the rectum. In Zambia the
Lord healed many through His healing gifts: two alcoholics were
set free; others were healed of different body aches including
stomach pains. One lady's goiter was drastically reduced and the
priest continues to pray with her for a complete healing. This is
"normal" Christianity! Glory to God!

The gifts of faith and miracles also work together powerfully
with the gifts of healing. A healing takes place gradually, but
a miracle is instantaneous. It takes charismatic faith to believe
God for a miracle. Jesus operated most of the time in miraculous
healings. These gifts are like muscles; they need to be exercised
for them to become strong. Hang around people that use the gifts,
for the gifts are more "caught" than "taught!" Faith is contagious!

Many people today flock to psychic healers, santeros, New Age
healing techniques, reiki healing, etc., because they haven't seen
the power of the Holy Spirit at work. Where there is a vacuum, the
enemy will try to infiltrate and take over. Let's not allow this to
keep happening! As God's people, it is our responsibility to rise up
in the power of the Holy Spirit and proclaim the glorious Gospel
of the Kingdom, demonstrating its power to save, heal and deliver.
The Lord promises to work with us and confirm the message with
results. (Mark 16:20). Alleluia! Let's pick up that "mantle of
healing" and run with it!

"...while God also bore witness by signs and wonders and
various miracles and by gifts of the Holy Spirit distributed
according to His own will." (Hebrews 2:4).

How to Access Your Healing

HEALING IN THE EUCHARIST

"I Am the Bread of Life." (John 6:48).

Jesus is the Eucharist. When we receive Jesus in the Eucharist, we are receiving all the healing benefits that He won in Calvary for us. In Mass, just before receiving Holy Communion, we even say,

"Lord, I am not worthy to receive you, but just say the Word and I shall be healed."

Allow Him to heal you of anything that needs healing in your soul and body. Believe that He wants you well and receive His healing by faith. It's Jesus that we are receiving, His body and blood, and He comes "with Healing in its wings" (Malachi 4: 2). When we drink His Blood, we are receiving life, because the Scriptures say that life is in the Blood (Leviticus 17: 11).

On the night of the Passover something amazing happened that we really don't pay much attention to; and maybe we should! Every Israelite household was commanded by the Lord to kill a lamb and "eat the flesh that night, roasted; with unleavened bread and bitter herbs they shall eat it" (Exodus 12: 8). This of course, points to the Eucharist, because Jesus is the "Lamb of God." So every household ate lamb that night and afterwards, when Moses led them out of Egypt, the Scriptures say that:

"...all of them were healthy and strong" (Psalm 105: 37b) (GNB).

God's people were healed as they ate the Passover lamb! They were all able to leave Egypt; not one remained behind because of sickness! "...six hundred thousand men on foot, besides women and children" left Egypt that night (Exodus 12: 37)! All were strong enough to get up and go! Miraculous! If God's people could all be healed by eating "regular" lamb, imagine us as we eat the real Lamb of God, Jesus the Son of God!

Last month while ministering in Tanzania, I started to sense a sore throat coming against me; immediately I prayed over myself, believing God's Word that "by His wounds I have been healed." When I received Holy Communion, by faith, I started to thank the Lord for the healing of my throat. Before I knew it, it was gone! Sickness and disease are not welcome guests in my body; I immediately reject them and start appropriating healing, which is part of my inheritance in Christ and a benefit of His Kingdom.

Listen carefully to what the Apostle Paul says in 1 Corinthians 11: 27-30:

> "Whoever, therefore, eats the bread or drinks the cup of the Lord in an unworthy manner will be guilty of profaning the body and Blood of the Lord. Let a man examine himself, and so eat of the Bread and drink of the cup. For any one who eats and drinks without discerning the body eats and drinks judgment upon Himself. That is why many of you are weak and ill, and some have died."

What exactly is an "unworthy manner?" It is not only not discerning the real presence of Jesus in the Eucharist, but also not discerning that the body of the Lord is also the people with whom you are receiving the Eucharist with. In other words, we are supposed to partake of Holy Communion in unity with the Lord and with our brothers and sisters. To receive the Eucharist unworthily is to receive Him disregarding the people around us. Are there divisions and factions? And where these exist, it usually comes accompanied with judgementalism, criticism, grumbling and complaining, anger, gossip, etc. Are you a source of unity or disunity? Do you create division, show favoritism, or ignore others? Jesus prayed six times in John 17 that we would be one! Unity in His people is very dear to the heart of Jesus! The Apostle Paul says in verse 18:

"...when you assemble as a church, I hear that there are divisions among you...."

What happens when we don't discern the body and we eat and drink the Lord's Supper in an unworthy manner? We become weak, ill, and might die; the opposite of what the Lord intended! That's why the Apostle Paul says to judge ourselves before we partake of the Lord's Supper (v.31). I believe that many people have become way too "familiar" with the Eucharist and for them it has become something casual or just another religious ritual. This could be deadly!

"Do not labor for the food which perishes, but for the food which endures to eternal life, which the Son of man will give to you; for on Him has God the Father set His seal." (John 8: 27).

RELEASE YOUR FAITH!

"And without faith it is impossible to please Him. For whoever would draw near to God must believe that He exists and that He rewards those who seek him." (Hebrews 11:6).

How do we please God? Through faith, and faith needs to be released, for "faith apart from works is dead." (James 2: 26). At times, "works" is turning to Jesus and speaking out what you believe in your heart. Faith has a "voice." Faith is for now; in heaven we will not need it! Faith demands some kind of action, not a passive response. We have in the Bible numerous examples of people getting healed as they released faith in the person of Jesus Christ. They spoke out; some even shouted! Some walked a long distance. And if you notice, Jesus never turned them down and they received their healing!

✦ in Matthew 8:2, the leper knelt before Jesus and told him "Lord, if you will, you can make me clean."

✦ in Matthew 8:8, the centurion told Jesus "…only say the word, and my servant will be healed."

✦ in Matthew 9:18, Jairus knelt before Jesus and told Him "…My Daughter has just died; but come and lay your hand on her, and she will live." Now, that's faith!

✦ in Matthew 9:21, the woman with the bleeding touched Jesus' garment as she said to herself, "If I only touch his garment, I shall be made well."

✦ in Matthew 15:22, a desperate Canaanite woman cried out to Jesus for her daughter's deliverance "Have mercy on me, O Lord, Son of David; my daughter is severely possessed by a demon."

✦ in Mark 10:47-48, blind Bartimeaus shouted and kept shouting, "Jesus, Son of David, have mercy on me!"

✦ in Luke 17:13, the ten lepers "lifted up their voices and said, Jesus, Master, have mercy on us."

In John 4:49, an official approached Jesus and told Him "Sir, come down before my child dies."

Jesus was rather happy when anyone approached Him in faith, even when it bothered the people around Him! He let them know and encouraged their faith:

"Truly, I say to you, not even in Israel have I found such faith." (Matthew 8: 10).

"...and when Jesus saw their faith He said to the paralytic...." (Matthew 9:2).

"Take heart, daughter; your faith has made you well." (Matthew 9:22).

"Then He touched their eyes, saying, According to your faith be it done to you". (Matthew 9:29).

"Then Jesus answered her, O woman, great is your faith! Be it done for you as you desire." (Matthew 15:28).

"And He said to him, Rise and go your way; your faith has made you well." (Luke 17:19).

How does faith come? Romans 10:17 says: "So faith comes from what is heard, and what is heard comes by the preaching of Christ." Besides this, God has given each one of us a measure of faith (Romans 12: 3). Faith is what moves the Lord to do something about the situation. Faith does not come by watching the soap operas or reading worldly magazines; on the contrary, your faith will suffer when you feed on the wrong things. If we want to walk in victory, we need to renew our minds daily with the Word of God. It takes a renewal of our minds in order to grasp what the Holy Spirit wants to accomplish in us and through us today. Romans 12:2 says,

"Do not be conformed to this world but be transformed by the renewal of your mind...."

It's through the Word of God that our minds are renewed so that we can think like He thinks. We need to destroy every stronghold in our minds and "arguments and every proud obstacle to the knowledge of God, and take every thought captive to obey Christ..." (2 Corinthians 10: 4-5). We need to start thinking like He thinks, so that we can carry on with His works! No wonder the enemy has convinced so many of God's children that the Scriptures are not that important. Ask the Lord to give you a desire for His Word, because it's not enough just to hear them read on Sundays! It's by faith that we appropriate His promises. Unbelief is not something that pleases God; the Scriptures calls unbelief evil! (Hebrews 3:12). Look at how important it is to release faith:

"For good news came to us just as to them;
But the message which they heard did not benefit them,
Because it did not meet with faith in the hearers."
(Hebrews 4:2).

III

Hindrances to Healing

Even though Jesus has already obtained our healing 2,000 years ago on the Cross of Calvary, we must appropriate this benefit by faith. The following are common hindrances that block our healing.

IGNORANCE

"My people are destroyed for lack of knowledge...."
(Hosea 4:6).

I believe that most people do not know that Jesus carried every sickness and disease on the Cross so that we could be healed. Many don't even know that as God's people we are supposed to lay hands on the sick for healing. Some people think that Jesus only healed when He walked physically on earth, but not today. Some people think that it is God who sends disease. As you see, our own man-made opinions about healing can keep us sick and in pain. What is important is what the Scriptures reveal about it. I believe that many people die before their time because nobody prayed for them. Ignorance can be deadly! No wander Jesus spent so much time teaching God's people!

Recently I received an e-mail from a young lady suffering from cancer, whom I've been in contact with through the e-mails. She e-mailed me when she read an article about "my ministry" and the healings I have seen. I wrote her back explaining what Jesus had done for her on the Cross, taking not only the sin and iniquity, but also every sickness and disease so that she could he healed. I gave her many scripture references for her to read and meditate on. In her last e-mail she wrote:

"So thank you soooooooooooo much for introducing me to this person, Jesus!! And for introducing me to this Good News, this Gospel. I always thought the "good news" part was just that we are saved from going to hell. Definitely very good news, the best news, but I thought it was limited to that, our destiny after we die. Thank you for opening me up to the reality that it isn't just after I die that I can take part in what Jesus accomplished for us on the Cross."

The Holy Spirit definitely gave this young lady revelation that there is healing today available for her, and now she is full of hope for the future! As a matter of fact, two days ago I received an e-mail from her saying that doctors have found no more trace of cancer! Alleluia!

"And every day He was teaching in the temple, but a night He went out and lodged on the mount called Olivet. And early in the morning all the people came to Him in the temple to hear Him." (Luke 21:37-38).

UNBELIEF

"And He could do no mighty work there, except He laid
his hands upon a few sick people and healed them. And He
marveled because of their unbelief." (Mark 6: 5-6).

Even Jesus was hindered because of unbelief. In His own
hometown He could not accomplish what He had wanted. He
could do no miracles there and only healed a few people. That's
why Jesus kicked the unbelievers out of the house of Jairus before
raising his daughter from the dead. Jesus told those that were
"weeping and wailing loudly,"

"Why do you make a tumult and weep? The child is not
dead but sleeping. And they laughed at him. But He put
them all outside...." (Mark 5:38-40).

Peter took the same action in Acts 9 before raising Dorcas from
the dead; he put all outside while he remained inside the room with
Dorcas. Peter prayed and just commanded Dorcas to rise up. And
she did! An atmosphere of unbelief can be deadly! The Israelites
could not possess the promised land (except for Joshua and Caleb)
because of unbelief:

"So we see that they were unable to enter because of
unbelief" (Hebrews 3:19). Remember, the Lord had
delivered them out of Egypt to bring them into the
promised land. That was His plan; but it got thwarted
because of their unbelief!

Often when I am asked to pray for a sick person in the
hospital, I kindly ask the visitors to leave the room; most of the
time they are in unbelief and it's difficult to minister in that kind
of atmosphere. Many churchgoers don't have faith in Jesus for
healing, even though they have faith in Him for salvation. Faith

comes by hearing; if they don't feed on the Scriptures and if they have never heard living testimonies of what the Holy Spirit still does today, they have no reason to believe.

Just today at the food store, the lady at the cash register was complaining of pain and discomfort due to high blood pressure. This lady was wearing a pin of the Virgin Mary, a rosary and a crucifix; you could tell she was a Catholic a mile away! I talked to her about Jesus the Healer and she looked at me like if I had lost my mind. Sadly enough, this is a very common response!

A neighbor of a teenager suffering from brain cancer asked us to go and pray for this young lady. She had many tumors in her brain; doctors had not given her much hope of a long life. We went over to her house, and we sensed a lot of anger and unbelief in the parents. They were angry at God for the sickness and had no faith in Him for healing. Through the revelation of a "word of knowledge" I knew there was involvement in Santeria. I asked her mother about it, and the mother replied that both the grandmother and herself had been involved in it. I explained to them the need for repentance and renunciation; I explained to them that the "fruit" of occultism in the generations often was sickness and disease in the children, but the mother flatly told me "I don't believe what you're telling me."

> "Truly, I say to you, unless you turn and become like children, you will never enter the kingdom of heaven." (Matthew 18: 3).

HIDDEN AND UNCONFESSED SIN

"He who conceals his transgressions will not prosper,
But he who confesses and forsakes them will obtain
mercy." (Proverbs 28:13).

Sin in our lives is an open door for the enemy to come into our
lives to kill, steal and destroy (John 10:10) with sickness and
disease. It's like leaving the back door of your house open!
Unwanted guests will probably pay you a visit! Even anger will
give the devil a foothold in our lives! (Ephesians 4:26-27). Some
people are sick because of an open door of sin in their lives. We
must be determined to leave sin behind. It's extremely important
that we shut the door to the enemy by renouncing, repenting and
confessing every sin, including any kind of occultic involvement in
the past. Remember, the power of the gospel includes the power to
leave sin behind and to walk in victory over it.

Many people don't pay much attention to involvement in the
occult; however, God considers it an abomination! It must be
renounced and repented of in order to receive forgiveness. That
open door needs to be shut! Occultism involves things such as
horoscopes, ouija boards, tarot cards, Santeria, spiritism, palm
reading, reike healing, new age philosophy, etc. And it must be
confessed even if you were doing it just for fun!

One lady in our prayer group was depressed and suffering from
migraines. I prayed with her and I sensed by the Spirit that she had
been involved in santeria (Cuban witchcraft). I asked her and she
said "No." Finally one day she "confessed" that indeed at a time
of great need she visited a santero, who gave her a potion to drink.
I had her renounce this activity and she repented. She "burped"
out those evil spirits that were lodging inside of her as soon as she
repented; she was set free! Thank you, Jesus!

Another older lady from our prayer group kept getting sick
every month, each time with something different. This lady
attended several prayer groups every week and attended every

healing Mass you could imagine.   One day when the Miami area was threatened with a hurricane, I invited her to stay with my family. We were roommates that night. To my surprise, very early in the morning she woke up and turned on her radio to a psychic healer, who answered many questions from the callers. I told my friend to turn that program off, for it was an abomination in the eyes of God. Her response was this: "Come on, Maria, everybody listens to this show." I knew right away this was connected to her getting sick so frequently! Eventually I gave her some pamphlets on the dangers of occultism; she read them, repented, went to confession. Afterwards she experienced a great peace and entered into better health. Thank you, Jesus!

Jesus told the man who received healing after thirty eight years of being ill, "Remember, now, you have been cured. Give up your sins so that something worse many not overtake you." (John 5: 14-15) (NAB).

Hindrances to Healing

UNFORGIVENESS

"Then Peter came up and said to Him, Lord, how often shall my brother sin against me, and I forgive him? As many as seven times? Jesus said to him, I do not say to you seven times, but seventy times seven." (Matthew 18: 21-22).

One of the biggest obstacles in the Church is unforgiveness. Jesus spoke very clearly on this subject: we must forgive whoever has harmed us or hurt us. This is basic to our faith as Christians! When we pray the "Our Father" we ask the Father to "forgive us our debts, as we also have forgiven our debtors..." (Matthew 6:12). He forgives us as we forgive others. The Apostle Paul says in Colossians 3:13

"...as the Lord has forgiven you, so you also must forgive."

Jesus says in Mark 11:25,

"And whenever you stand praying, forgive, if you have anything against any one; so that your Father also who is in heaven may forgive you your trespasses."

Unforgiveness is another open door to the enemy, who only comes to try to destroy us in any way that he can, causing mental anguish, emotional problems and physical illnesses. This door must be closed if we want to walk in victory in this life. In Matthew 18:23-35, Jesus says that if we don't forgive, His Father Himself will deliver us to the "torturers." (NAB). Being tortured is no fun! What do "torturers" do? They torture with sickness, disease, panic attacks, anxiety, confusion, fear, to name a few.

While in Tanzania, we visited a Catholic orphanage of teenage girls. We praised the Lord, danced and were joyful in His presence. In the natural the girls looked happy; many had been baptized in the Holy Spirit and spoke in tongues. After I gave my testimony and moved in words of knowledge for healings, I knew that many of those young ladies needed to forgive. When I said "Some of you need to forgive," many started to wail; you could hear the loud wailings across the room! As soon as the Holy Spirit started to go a little deeper, He revealed a big but hidden problem in the girls: unforgiveness. By the grace of God, some were able to forgive and experienced physical and inner healing.

Just today my brother, who is a doctor, treated a 75-year-old woman suffering from arthritis and sciatic pain; she was in great pain. My brother realized by a word of knowledge that this lady had not forgiven those who had hurt her. The Holy Spirit, the Spirit of truth and revelation, was right on target. My brother prayed with her and she repented, committed her life to Jesus and forgave those who had hurt her. Her body pains left her body and she left his office thanking Jesus! Alleluia!

My dear brothers and sisters, God's grace is available for you to forgive. Make that decision, make that choice to forgive. Don't focus on your feelings, but take that step of faith to forgive all. Speak it out! Let the enemy know that you're not in "cahoots" with him anymore! One thing that I do, is not only forgive, but I start blessing those people that have hurt me. This is one way to overcome evil with good. The Apostle Paul says,

"Do not be overcome by evil, but overcome evil with good." (Romans 12: 21).

CURSES

"…a curse that is causeless does not alight." (Proverbs 26: 2).

We see from this Scripture that when there is a curse, there is a reason for the curse being there: sin and iniquity. (Please check out the list of curses that can come upon us because of disobedience in Deuteronomy 28:15-68). Unconfessed sin and iniquity in the family tree, in which there has been no repentance and forgiveness, gives the enemy a legal right to enforce a curse in the descendants. My definition of a curse is a negative, powerful force coming down the family tree: it's demonic. As it relates to sickness or disease, when you see a sickness repeated throughout the generations, or if you see it many times in one generation, that's a good indication that a curse might be present. For example, at times you see cancer repeated down the family tree; depression, alcoholism, diabetes, etc., tend to run in families. Even doctors will ask you to fill out a form with your "family history" of sickness and disease. The curse needs to be broken before the healing can take place. One thing that definitely releases a curse in a family is idolatry and involvement in the occult:

"You shall have no other gods before me. You shall not make for yourself a graven image, or any likeness of anything that is in heaven above, or that is in the earth beneath, or that is in the water under the earth; you shall not bow down to them or serve them; for I the lord your God am a jealous God, visiting the iniquity of the fathers upon the children to the third and the fourth generation of those who hate me…." (Exodus 20: 3-5).

From this passage of Scripture we see that a curse can visit the family to the third and fourth generation. How can a curse be broken? We turn to Jesus! He made provision on the Cross so that curses could be broken and we could walk in freedom. Galatians

3:13 says,

> "Christ redeemed us from the curse of the law, having
> become a curse for us—for it is written, "Cursed is every
> one who hangs on a tree"—that in Christ Jesus the blessing
> of Abraham might come upon the Gentiles...."

On the Cross of Calvary, Jesus became a curse for us so that
the curse could be broken and we could enter into the blessings
of Abraham, "whom God blessed in every way." (Genesis 24: 1).
The first thing that we need to do is to repent and ask the Lord for
forgiveness for whatever sin and iniquity has caused this curse to
be there. Sometimes we don't know what has caused the curse;
the Holy Spirit knows, ask Him! Trust the Lord that even if you
don't know what caused the curse, you can still break it in faith
by repenting and asking for forgiveness. After a curse is broken
(by faith), start proclaiming the opposite with your mouth. For
example, if there has been alcoholism, start proclaiming sobriety
in your descendants; if there has been a history of depression, start
proclaiming the joy of the Lord in your family.

In my family tree there is diabetes on both sides; both my
parents were diabetic and two of my grandparents as well. At one
point I was diagnosed as a pre-diabetic; the doctor told me that
probably I would become diabetic later on in life. I have broken
that curse in my life and today I am not a diabetic. Thank you,
Jesus!

I have broken many curses coming from my family tree;
however, the Holy Spirit keeps revealing new ones. For example,
on my last trip to Uganda in 2006, as I woke up very early one
morning to get ready for the day's mission, I could hardly get
out of bed. I was experiencing a dizziness that was making me
nauseas; the whole room seemed to be spinning out of control.
This was similar to something I had experienced way back in 1992,
only a hundred times worse! I realized that I had been cursed by
a witch doctor; I just knew it by the Spirit. This was confirmed by

other members of the team and also by my brother back home. I
asked the Lord to show me why this had happened. The Holy
Spirit reminded me that my mother used to suffer from dizziness.
I also found out that my father and grandmother suffered from it
also. In addition, my brother also had suffered with vertigo on two
occasions. I realized this was a "family" thing: a curse! Because
this curse had never been broken, the enemy had a "legal right"
to enforce it! You see, the devil is a "legal expert." As long as
that curse remained unbroken, the enemy had a right to enforce it.
Naturally, I have broken the curse of dizziness and vertigo over my
life and have prayed for healing. I am getting healed progressively
as I aggressively take over my inheritance of healing. Amen!

We have prayed with several women that were unable to
conceive children, and after breaking curses of barrenness, they've
conceived and have borne children successfully. We have also
prayed with some that kept having miscarriages, and after the
breaking of a curse they have been able to carry the baby full term.
Thank you, Jesus! We prayed for a young mother who had two
girls; there was a family history of problems at child birth in her
family tree. Both girls were born with health problems and had
to be placed in neo-natal units in the hospital until healed. When
this young mother got pregnant again, we broke curses over her
life dealing with childbirth and her baby boy was born completely
healthy. This is a testimony of the power of the Holy Spirit to
release the promises of God's healing and restoration to His
people.

Today in many charismatic circles there are Masses being
celebrated for the healing of the family tree. All of us need
generational healing and cleansing! Amen!

"Cursed be he who does not confirm the words of this
law by doing them. And all the people shall say, Amen."
(Deuteronomy 27: 26).

WRONG DIAGNOSIS: IT'S DEMONIC IN ORIGIN

"As they were going away, behold, a dumb demoniac was brought to him. And when the demon had been cast out, the dumb man spoke; and the crowds marveled, saying, 'Never was anything like this seen in Israel.'" (Matthew 9:32-33).

As you see from this passage, a spirit had to be cast out from this man in order to be freed and healed. It wasn't speech therapy that helped him! The root of the problem was demonic; Jesus knew it and dealt with it. As a matter of fact, He said that the casting out of demons signified that "the kingdom of God has come upon you." (Matthew 12:28).

In Matthew 17, there is the story of the epileptic boy whom the disciples couldn't help, even though they tried. The father of the boy told Jesus "...I brought him to your disciples, and they could not heal him." (v.16). Jesus ministered to the boy:

"And Jesus rebuked him, and the demon came out of him, and the boy was cured instantly." (v. 18).

As you see, Jesus had to rebuke the demon first, for the boy to be set free and healed. Once again, we see that the root of the problem in this boy's health was demonic; Jesus dealt directly with the problem and the boy was healed instantly.

Another example of bringing freedom and healing to the captives is the woman that was bent over, which Jesus found in the synagogue (not under the bridge!). It says in Luke 13:11 that this woman "had a spirit of infirmity for eighteen years; she was bent over and could not fully straighten herself." It was a spirit of infirmity that had kept this woman miserable for eighteen years. Something happened when Jesus saw her....

"...He called her and said to her, "Woman, you are freed

from your infirmity. And He laid His hands upon her, and immediately she was made straight, and she praised God." (Luke 13:12-13).

The ruler of the synagogue was very upset because Jesus had healed on the Sabbath. Jesus called him "hypocrite" and also told him:

"And ought not this woman, a daughter of Abraham whom Satan bound for eighteen years, be loosed from this bond on the Sabbath day?"

The point that I am trying to make is that still today, the root of some sicknesses could be demonic in origin and this is the reason why the person is not getting healed. We have been gifted with the gift of discernment of spirits that reveals to us if the person needs deliverance. My mother, who was a psychiatrist, realized after she was baptized in the Holy Spirit, that the root of the problems in many of her patient's problems were demonic in origin. Medicine, in many cases, could only deal with the symptoms; the real problem, an evil spirit(s), needed to be cast out in the name of Jesus for the person to be healed.

I have lost count of the times in which I am praying with people for healing and there are demonic manifestations! It is not the purpose of this book on healing to give details of such encounters; it is the purpose of this chapter to make you aware that the root cause of a person's sickness could be demonic and it needs to be dealt with if the person is to be freed and healed. Amen!

My brother, the doctor, ministered to a "Catholic" lady patient who had suffered from left side abdominal pain for over 20 years. She had been tested and treated by different gastroenterologists with no results. As my brother prayed with her, he asked the Lord for a word of knowledge to get to the root of the problem. The Lord gave him the word "San Lazaro," which is a Santeria, witchcraft "saint." My brother commanded the spirit of "San

Lazaro" to leave her; it came out and the pain was gone! She was
set free from the pain and then told my brother that all her life
she had placed "San Lazaro" above Jesus. This lady renounced
Santeria, repented and gave her life to Jesus. This is a powerful
example of the gift of word of knowledge to set the captives free.
Medicine could not heal this lady because the root of the problem
was demonic.

On another occasion my brother was treating an 80-year-old
lady with fibromyalgia. She was barely able to function. My
brother commanded the spirit of fibromyalgia to leave her and
declared her totally healed in her joints, bones and muscles.
Immediately she ran and jumped without any pain!

I want to share with you my friend Jill's story:

"I was experiencing chest pains in the middle of my back
that pushed through to the front. I spoke to my doctor about the
problem and he ran an E.K.G. He seemed puzzled and said he
saw a problem and wanted to check with the cardiologist across
the hall from him. He came back and said he wanted me to have
some more tests. An ultrasound and a stress test were ordered. My
stress test was scheduled to be performed in three weeks. After I
came home from the doctor's office I looked at the paper they gave
me and the doctor had written on the paper C.A.D and L.V.F. I
later found out that C.A.D. was coronary artery disease and L.V.F.
was left ventricular function. A few days later, while I was doing
my daily walk, I experienced a sharp pain and had to stop walking.
I came home and my husband knew by the look on my face
something was wrong. He insisted we go to the E.R. just to be on
the safe side. Once we were at the hospital my pains were getting
worse. At the hospital I was given nitroglycerin and it helped with
the chest pain, so the staff was sure I was having heart problems. I
was told I needed to spend a few days in the hospital. That night,
the nurse came in and said to my husband and me, 'I see you are
Christians; may I pray with you?' We were more than happy to
have her pray with us. This woman was a real prayer warrior and
very knowledgeable in spiritual warfare. She put her hand on my

chest and she commanded the spirit of death to leave me. She came against the curses of heart attack, C.A.D. and L.V.F. and commanded them to leave me. We refused to accept the doctor's diagnosis, declaring Isaiah 54:17,"

"No weapon that is formed against you will prosper, and every tongue that accuses you in judgment you will condemn. This is the heritage of the servants of the Lord, and their vindication is from Me," declares the Lord."

"We commanded the spirits that were on assignment to those words that were formed against me, to leave in Jesus' name. We declared that the words that were spoken over my life and the words that were written, (the demonic prophecy over my life!), C.A.D. and L.V.F., were now cancelled and would come to nothing. Had we not done this, those words would most likely have come into existence. My husband and the nurse together went to war against the powers of darkness and called the spirits that were trying to kill me to come out in the name of Jesus. We also called the spirit of jealousy out, since it is also a killer. When an evil spirit leaves a person it comes out on your breath: yawning, belching, tearing, sneezing, vomiting. (They even come out through diarrhea and passing gas). After the prayers I was so sick that I was yawning every few minutes for about 15 to 20 minutes, and my whole body shook as I yawned. I started vomiting and had diarrhea. I felt so sick that all I wanted was to get this out of me. I even got a soda from the soda machine so I could drink it fast and belch. Now that I look back on it I am sure I was delivered of demons of death and heart disease. The next day I had a stress test and the doctors could find nothing wrong. I have a normal, healthy heart with nothing wrong, because we went into spiritual warfare in Jesus' name."

"And these signs will accompany those who believe: in my name they will cast out demons...." (Mark 16:17).

Healing is for You!

IV

The Children's Bread -
Healing Testimonies

"But she came and knelt before Him, saying, "Lord, help
me." And He answered, "It is not fair to take the children's
bread and throw it to the dogs." She said, "Yes, Lord, yet
even the dogs eat the crumbs that fall from their master's
table." Matthew 15:25-27.

From this passage we see that Jesus referred to healing and
deliverance as the children's bread. Bread is a daily, common,
everyday food on our tables. Jesus is saying that for God's
children, healing and deliverance are a regular part of our diets!
Let's leave behind the "crumbs mentality" and know that He is
"able to do far more abundantly than all that we ask or think…."
(Ephesians 3:20). Jesus says in Matthew 7:7-11,

"Ask, and it will be given you; seek, and you will find;
Knock, and it will be opened to you. For every one who
asks receives, and he who seeks finds, and to him who
knocks it will be opened. Or what man of you, if his son
asks him for bread, will give him a stone? Or if he asks
for a fish, will give him a serpent? If you then, who are
evil, know how to give good gifts to your children, how
much more will your Father who is in heaven give good
things to those who ask Him!"

Healing is indeed not only a good thing, but a wonderful thing.
The Lord Himself encourages us to ask, seek and knock!   Here

are testimonies of God's children receiving the "bread" of healing. Some of the healings are instant and others are progressive; but notice the different ways in which God's people have been healed. Let's not place Him in a box, but let's be open to the guidance of the Holy Spirit to receive and release the healing of the kingdom.

1. Ina's testimony:

"My grandson Carlos was diagnosed with a hearing deficiency and a speech impediment at age two. For five years he repeatedly received prayer ministry with the laying on of hands. We saw little change in his condition, but I did not stop praying for him, believing that 'by His wounds' my grandson was already healed. One day in the prayer group we started to break generational curses and that's when his breakthrough came. The healing started to manifest and Carlos did not need surgery to fix the problem. Today he's a normal child getting ready to enter into junior high school."

2. Ani's testimony:

"My son Jose was diagnosed with learning disability and auditory processing deficiency at age five. He couldn't learn like everybody else. He couldn't connect between what he saw and what he heard. I had to place him in a special school. I started to study the Word of God and realized that there's healing in Jesus and that I could actually pray over my son and lay hands on him. I immediately started to lay hands on him (also on his pillow!) and pray and declare that 'My son has the mind of Christ.' There was an immediate change! The teacher asked me if I had placed Jose on medication because his ability to learn was really improving. In less than a year I was able to change my son to a regular school. Today he's an A-B student in eighth grade getting ready for regular high school."

3. Celina's testimony:

"In the 13th week of my fourth pregnancy, I found out that I was carrying monoamniotic twins. Monoamniotic twins are in the same sac and this caused my pregnancy to be labeled not just high risk, as my OB said, but VERY high risk. The biggest risk was that the cords would become tangled and compressed, causing the death of one or both babies. There was also the risk of twin to twin transfusion syndrome. After the attending perinatologist at the ultrasound visit described all the risks, he suggested that we might want to consider abortion. We quickly turned down his offer.

I have to admit that I was not immediately optimistic that God would see us through this. As I researched online, I found many articles documenting a 50% chance of both twins surviving. I wallowed in fear and anxiety for about 2 days before God stepped in and pulled me out of my misery. He stepped in with a series of 'Godincidences' that began with my Bible reading that day. I had been reading one to two Psalms a day as part of my morning prayer before getting the children ready for school. On this particular day, I read Psalms 33 and 34. As I was reading them, I suddenly felt God's power and what His power could do for my babies and for me. I had heard everything that I was reading before, but it really touched my heart on that morning. Psalm 34:4 became especially meaningful to me and I would repeat it many times during my pregnancy:

'I sought the Lord who answered me and delivered me from all my fears.'

Later that morning, my husband and I received words of encouragement from a Spirit-filled couple who we 'bumped into' at Mass. Note that this was a weekday and I couldn't remember if I had EVER seen both of them at morning Mass

TOGETHER before. I would usually see one but not the other and it was a blessing to hear their own testimony of a risky pregnancy from both of them.

On that same day, my OB explained that my pregnancy was too high risk for me to deliver at the hospital he was associated with. I would have to find another doctor. This was no easy task since it is now rare to find a perinatologist (high-risk obstetrician) in our area who will deliver babies. The majority of them now operate in a consulting mode and monitor your pregnancy together with your regular OB who will be the one to finally deliver. I was determined that I wanted to see just one doctor for both pre-natal and delivery. Through 3 separate 'Godincidences' on that day, 3 separate people highly recommended the same doctor who fit my requirements. Everyone told me that it would be very difficult to get an appointment with this doctor but God opened the doors for me and I got an appointment within 2 weeks. This doctor turned out to be just what I needed. She was a very tough and blunt doctor and had contributed to a book on guidelines for a healthy multiple pregnancy. (The average OB is not aware of these special guidelines for multiple pregnancies). She had me follow the weight gain guidelines in the book plus take multiple pills. She limited the times I could go upstairs since I live in a 2-story house. I know and God knows I needed a doctor with a strong personality and a book with well-documented research to convince me to follow all the recommendations. Yet this was not the doctor who saw my pregnancy to the end.

In my 26th week, she left private practice and transferred my case to another perinatologist who had a gentle and accommodating disposition, perfect for the end of my pregnancy. God is so wise! This doctor prayed for me and, of course, he knew how high the risks were for me. I later found out he was treating another woman with my condition who lost both twins at 16 weeks during my own pregnancy. I finally delivered the babies by C-section with this praying doctor without any incidents or complications.

I know that all these events transpired because I trusted what God revealed to me in Psalms 33 and 34. I read those Psalms virtually every day of the remainder of my pregnancy. Not only were the words in those Psalms meaningful to me, but the numbers also became meaningful to me. My doctor told me that I would have the babies at 34 weeks. The risks of staying in the womb outweighed the risks of being born at 34 weeks. Well, I was very afraid of delivering that early. But I went to Mass one weekday struggling with that fear and God again delivered me from my fears. The alleluia verse, the priest's sermon (yes, how often do you get a sermon in a weekday Mass?) and finally the communion song which was from Psalm 34 confirmed that God was in agreement with delivery at 34 weeks. I actually delivered the babies 2 days before the humanly planned date, exactly at 34 weeks! That was God showing me once again that He was calling the shots! Now that wasn't enough for Him; one of the babies was born at 9:34 and the Psalm in the Sunday Mass after the birth was from Psalm 33. Coincidences? I don't think so; more like 'Godincidences!'

Many people prayed for me during my pregnancy, including Maria who laid hands on my growing belly weekly. My husband and I prayed every night with our other 3 children. We asked God to make the twins grow big and strong, especially when I knew I only had until the 34th week . God delivered me from the fear of having small, underweight preemies. Psalm 34:10 says:

'Nothing is lacking to those who fear Him.'

The twins were born at 5 lbs. 2 oz. and 5 lbs. This is the same weight expected in the 34th week of a singleton pregnancy. We continued praying for them to grow bigger and fatter, and at their 1 year checkup, they were both above the 99th percentile for height and weight based on their age (i.e. not adjusted by their pre-mature birth)! Our other 3 children were never so high on the growth charts. It pleased God to reveal His glory and answer our prayers by making the twins enormous!

About the threat of cord entanglement, we knew the cords were tangled by the 20th week. There is nothing you can do to detangle the cords or to keep them from getting compressed to the point of killing 1 or both babies. We simply had to trust that God would keep the babies safe. Psalm 33:18-19 says,

'But the Lord's eyes are upon the reverent, upon those who hope for His gracious help, delivering them from death.'

By the time the twins were born, the cords were VERY tangled, but to the glory of God, this had not compromised their health or their growth one bit!"

4. Gilda's testimony:

"My daughter Carolina went to her annual checkup with the gynecologist. The doctor examined her and told her that he felt an enlarged ovary. The next day she had a sonogram done and was told that she had a double cyst in her ovary. In other words, she had a cyst inside of another cyst. The sonogram clearly showed that there was a solid mass in her ovary. She was sent to a surgeon, who explained that most probably she would lose part of that ovary. I spent the night before the surgery praying for healing for my daughter. My friends came just before leaving for the hospital and laid hands on Carolina and prayed for healing, taking authority over the cysts and commanding them to disappear. When the surgeon operated, all he found was a water cyst!"

5. Gilda's testimony:

"I was bleeding from one of my nipples and was sent to a specialist. He told me I would need surgery to remove some ducts from my breast. My friends prayed and laid hands on me just before surgery. I was on the surgical bed with the hospital gown on and ready for the surgery, when the surgeon checked my breast and said "I can't operate because whatever you had is gone.""

6. Graciela's testimony:

"When I was pregnant with my baby I was diagnosed with cancerous cells in my uterus. Three consecutive tests confirmed this. I immediately cried out to the Lord; I could not believe this was happening to me! For many years I had desired to be married and have a family... and now that I was expecting my first baby, here I was, diagnosed with cancer! The Holy Spirit reminded me of Mark 11:14, where Jesus cursed the fruitless fig tree. I started to curse the root of the cancerous cells so that they would wither and die. My friends laid hands on me, prayed in tongues, cursed the root of the cancerous cells and declared a complete healing in my uterus. I knew that I was healed. I was scheduled for a biopsy even while pregnant, because the doctor said this couldn't wait. I didn't want this procedure to be done, because I thought it would affect the baby. However, the baby came three weeks early, and it was several months after her birth that I was tested. There was no trace of cancerous cells in my uterus. I thank the Lord for His healing; all glory and honor to the Lord Jesus Christ!"

7. Aida's testimony:

"My mother had a spur on her foot and she was in a lot of pain.

She had seen me pray over the children, my dad and other persons, and she asked me if I would pray for her. What made this so different is that while I was praying I could actually feel the spur disappear and she felt it too. She hasn't had a problem since. Praise Jesus Christ!"

8. Debbie's testimony (not her real name):

"My name is Debbie. I am 51 years old and for most of my life I lived in a daze. I was covered with shame and guilt, pain and fear, that the sin of abortion and sexual immorality brought into my life. I even tried to take my own life several times, but God was gracious to me. When I received the Lord Jesus Christ as my Lord and Savior back in 2000 led in prayer by Maria Vadia, my life started to change. The Holy Spirit revealed to me that there were many areas of my life that I needed to surrender to Him. I started to go to King Jesus prayer group and Bible Study Fellowship and the Word of God began to work in my heart and every fiber of my being. As I began to be convicted of what I had done to my children, I repented and asked the Lord to please forgive me. Because I felt the Mercy, Grace and Forgiveness of the Lord, I was able in turn to forgive all of those involved in my abortions and especially to forgive myself. I named my children and asked the Lord to tell them that I loved them and was able recently to attend a service for them and light candles on their behalf.

The only way that I have been able to survive the shame and be healed by the Lord is by having a CLOSE, INTIMATE RELATIONSHIP WITH JESUS CHRIST. It has not been by the things I do or the ministries I serve, or how many times I go to Church during the week......It has been by laying my heart out to the Lord, allowing Him to break it and restore it. It has not been easy, it has not been fun. It has taken many tears, but the Lord holds them in a vial. I had to be broken and realize that I was broken, so that I could be restored to love Him more than anything. I had to be quiet, I had to be still, I had to be alone, I had to cry out, but my tears were not wasted, and hope was restored. In God's Grace there is healing, and the healing comes by the power of His Word made flesh, Jesus Christ, our Lord. Amen."

9. Dr. Rene's testimony:

"I have a patient that was involved in New Age, Buddhism, yoga and eastern style meditation. She always turned down my offer to pray for her in Jesus' name. However, she was diagnosed with a cancerous tumor on her lung. During her pre-operation visit in my office, she finally agreed to receive prayer. I declared that the surgeon would not find any tumor. That's exactly what happened! There was no tumor! She then gave her life to Jesus and received Him as Lord and Savior."

10. Dr. Rene's testimony:

"One of my patients was devastated because her daughter, who lives in Brazil, had been diagnosed with metastatic breast cancer. The doctors in Brazil told her she had less than a year to live; she went ahead and bought her own burial plot and coffin. That day in the office I commanded the spirit of cancer to leave her in Jesus' name and prayed for total healing. Her mother and I had an inner assurance that her daughter was healed. The mother called her in Brazil and told her to go back to the doctor, for she was cancer free. The daughter did so, and after testing there was no trace of cancer in her body. She went ahead and sold her burial plot and coffin!"

11. Dolores' testimony:

" As a mother of ten children, you can imagine it has been stressful! Having as many as four in diapers all at once, I rarely had time to take care of myself and neglected to eat nutritional meals. By the time I was 52 years old with five children still living at home, I didn't realize how unhealthy I was.

After a very stressful Christmas three years ago, my two sons, Jesse, 18 years old, and Andrew, 21 years old, got in a terrible fight. I jumped between them and got a paralyzing pain in my chest and I fell to the ground. It felt like someone had hit me with a taser gun. I had had a heart attack. I tried to go to the hospital, but both hospitals were so crowded with an epidemic flu that there was no room. We left and I told God Almighty He was going to have to heal me. Over the next couple of weeks I prayed healing scriptures like '...by Your stripes I am healed' (1 Peter 2:24). Slowly I regained my strength but still was in a great deal of pain; each time my heart beat it was painful and irregular. I knew if I could go to the prayer meeting and enter into the presence of God through worship and ask for prayer, I would receive healing from the laying on of hands. That's exactly what I did.

As I was being prayed over, I felt the rush of the Holy Spirit and something gently touching my heart; immediately the pain left. After the prayer meeting a woman came up to me and said, 'Wow, did you see the beam of light hit your chest with a hand reaching into your heart?' The lady confirmed what I already knew, for the prophetic word spoken over me was that God was giving me a new heart.

The next day I realized I was not 100% healed yet; I asked God 'Why?' He showed me that there were changes I would need to make. I would have to rely on Him for strength and not on caffeine. Jesus told me I was going to have to start saying 'No' to my children. Compromising with them had been causing too much stress in my life. Jesus also told me He appointed me to be their parent, not their friend. So, I had a lot of changes to make, strongholds that Jesus would help me tear down. At this point, I had to receive weekly prayer at our King

Jesus prayer meeting. And each week the little bit of pressure I was feeling got less and less and is no more. Praise God all pain and anxiety have left me, no more panic attacks!"

12. Valli's testimony:

"In the early 1990's I experienced the worst asthma attack ever. I remember stooping over in my bedroom and bathroom, gasping for air and wondering when I was going to have to be admitted to the hospital for the too-often occurring attacks. Thankfully, that day my prayers and an inhaler that I always had handy, brought the terrible experience to an end. Several weeks later I was attending a Charismatic Conference in Miami. The priest or lay preacher who was leading us through the healing service spoke with the authority of Jesus and began calling out the words of knowledge regarding healing. When he said, 'Someone here is being healed right now of asthma; you can feel it lifting out of your chest area, as your lungs and bronchials are being healed.' I knew that all things are possible for God and that Jesus was my Healer. As I began to think along those lines, I sensed the Holy Spirit breathing into my lungs and a tremendous opening in my chest area, as I exhaled what I knew was the condition I had suffered with for many years. New life, new strength, and new hope were filling me. I had believed and received my healing! It was as though a balloon was being inflated inside of my diaphragm, as I was being delivered from the asthma. When the speaker asked for anyone experiencing this healing to come forward, I flew up front, running and rejoicing and claiming the healing power of my Lord and Savior Jesus Christ. Praise be to Him! I have never suffered such attacks since. He is the air I breathe—my all in all!"

13. Valli's testimony:

"When my Dad died in November of 1981, I remember being sorry that I had not been there in New York. I attended his funeral and flew back to Miami. Several weeks later, as I was driving home from work in December, I thought about the lacks in our relationship—how as a little girl, I never had that warm sit-in-his-lap kind of relationship that I saw my other friends had with their dads. Our Dad was a very tough man who always seemed angry, hurtful, striking out verbally against my Mom and us, just never happy unless he was at work. His smiles were seldom and few. As I drove, I started angrily dialoguing with the Lord and asked Him why He took my Dad before he had the opportunity to live a happy, loving life. I questioned if he could be in heaven, or on his way. How would he spend eternity?

Suddenly, traveling at an average speed in my car, out of the corner of my eye I noticed the blur of Christmas lights; and the dialogue with Jesus continued. I sensed Him saying to me in these very words, 'Do you remember every Christmas how your Dad would get your brother on the roof, insisting that he help put up the lights?' 'Yes, Lord,' I responded. Then He proceeded to tell me that he did that each year because the birth of the Savior was important to him.

Jesus reminded me that, because of my Italian immigrant father's strong Catholic upbringing, he insisted that we children go to Catholic school and attend Mass on Sundays. I learned so much about my faith there. Because he was brought up in a very poor (money-wise) family, the opportunity to work as a commercial fisherman became the fulfillment of his American dream. With a sixth grade education, he built a large fishing business in our home town of Freeport, NY, and was known as a good and honest businessman, as well as a faithful husband and father. He never showed much loving emotion, probably because his upbringing was very harsh and times were very hard. I was given compassion for him that day.

Thoughts and words from the Spirit of God flooded my mind and my heart, as the Lord continued to show me the good things that I could be grateful for in my father, confirming his love for me. The final revelation I had that day was that no one created by God ever fulfills all the plans He has for them and I should stop judging my Dad and instead give thanks for his life. The Lord had used him and my Mom to bring me into this awesome world. From that day forward, I was healed from resentment towards my Dad. About a week later, I had a dream and saw my Dad fishing on a heavenly canal with the broadest smile ever! Now I am truly able to honor my Father, to thank God for him, and to love him with all my heart. I look forward to heavenly embraces from him one day!"

14. Gale's testimony:

"My life changed forever on April 18th, 2003. I measure every event in my life as being before or after that day. It's the day a vehicle struck me from behind as I was making a transaction at an outdoor ATM in front of a grocery store. The woman who was driving the car jumped the curb, ran up on the sidewalk and pinned me against the wall, crushing my right leg and slamming my face and body into the storefront. The pain was excruciating, and prolonged, because the driver did not have the presence of mind to reverse the car to release me. I frantically gestured and yelled, 'Back up!' as did many of the store's customers who were watching the horrific scene. To no avail the woman continued to depress the car's accelerator. I called out, pleading to God, 'God, please help me.' At that instant, the car released me. Months later when I read the police report of the accident, I learned that customers from the store had pulled the driver out of the vehicle and reversed the car themselves.

'The Lord is near to all who call on Him' (Psalm 145:18).

Thank you, Lord, for moving those people to respond in action!

Once the car released me, I fell flat on my back. On the way down to the hard concrete, I remember thinking 'it's gonna hurt when I land,' and then being surprised and relieved when it felt as though a feather bed had caught me. The next thing I remember is a kind gentleman calling my name and holding my hand. He encouraged me to stay awake because the blood loss was too great, and he told me that he would stay with me until the paramedics arrived. A year later I spoke to witnesses of the accident who told me there had never been a man sitting, holding my hand or talking to me at any time. I now believe this encounter was with an angel of the Lord who ministered to me on that fateful day.

When the paramedics arrived, they told me that the injuries I sustained were life-threatening. In addition to multiple open fractures, extensive muscle, tendon, ligament and nerve damage, a major artery in my leg had been severed. I was bleeding to death. I was to be air-lifted by medi-vac to a local trauma hospital. I listened to a paramedic give an account of my condition over a hand-held radio who described my leg as a 90% amputation.

At that point, as I lay on the earth looking up at the sky, I completely surrendered my life into God's hands. I found strength and comfort in God's Holy Spirit. God promised me right then and there that I would live through this, and I would not lose my leg. 'God is our refuge and strength, an ever-present help in trouble' (Psalm 46:1). God promises that no matter how difficult the situation, He is with us. 'Never will I leave you; never will I forsake you' (Hebrews 13:5). Jesus tells us, 'Surely I Am with you always, to the very end of the age' (Matthew 28:20). 'Even to your old age and gray hairs I am He, I am He who will sustain you, I have made you and I will carry you; I will sustain you and I will rescue you' (Isaiah 46:4).

When I got to the hospital, the trauma physicians told me

that my injuries were very severe and that in all likelihood it would be necessary to amputate my leg. I instructed them to save my leg, trusting literally and figuratively God's promise, 'We walk by faith, not by sight' (2 Corinthians 5:7).
I spent nearly two months in the hospital. The doctors told me that I was a medical miracle...there were no other cases of patients with injuries similar to mine whose leg had been saved from amputation. Thank You, Lord, for saving mine, even thought it wasn't easy! During that time I had approximately seven surgeries and existed on round-the-clock cocktails of the most potent pain medications available. The level of pain I experienced, even on the meds, is indescribable. There were some very dark days. Thankfully, the presence of the Lord was close at hand. I couldn't rely on my own strength to see me through that period of time, so God supplied me with His strength. 'I can do all things through Christ who strengthens me' (Phillipians 4:13). God said to me, 'My grace is sufficient for you, for my power is made perfect in weakness' (2 Corinthians 12:9).

I also have to thank and credit my wonderful husband, beautiful daughter, who was five years old at the time, loving parents and brother, and other very caring family members and friends with providing me with unconditional love and support that helped sustain me through that difficult time and the trying times that were to come.

I was discharged from the hospital with a huge metal contraption called a fixator on my entire leg and was bound to a wheelchair. The doctors didn't know if I would ever get out of that wheelchair and ambulate on my own again, but I had faith that God had His own plans for me. In fact, almost a year to the day of my accident I attended a prayer group and met a faith-filled woman who had seen my accident and prayed over me that day. The entire prayer group had been praying for me throughout the year, without ever even knowing my name! I am living proof that the power of prayer is tremendous!

Healing is for You!

It's been almost four years since the accident. I have had approximately 14 surgeries, years of physical therapy and have gone from wheelchair to walker to crutches to cane and back again many times. Today I walk unassisted! Thank You, Lord, for healing me! Although I continue to have some physical limitations, if you saw me walking down the street, you would not realize that I was ever seriously disabled. I claim the promise in Isaiah 53:5 that by Jesus' wounds we are healed. It has truly been a physical, emotional, psychological and spiritual journey of healing. God was even gracious enough to grant me the love and mercy to forgive the woman who hit me. 'Bear with each other and forgive whatever grievances you may have against one another. Forgive as the Lord forgave you' (Colossians 3:13).

I am also very grateful for the many caring professionals and courageous patients I have befriended on this journey. Many who have watched me have commented on how strong a person I am and how positive my attitude seems. To them, my reply is that I have the greatest healer of all, Jesus Christ. My faith in Jesus and the personal relationship I have with Him allow me to function over my circumstances, not under them. Jesus gives me peace and joy which transcend my circumstances and transform my heart and mind. 'Do not be anxious about anything, but in everything, by prayer and petition, with thanksgiving, present your requests to God. And the peace of God which transcends all understanding, will guard your hearts and your minds in Christ Jesus' (Phillipians 4:6-7). The psalmist wrote, 'He is my loving God and my fortress...in whom I take refuge' (Psalm 144:2). I learned to trust each day into God's hands and to take it as a gift from Him. To Him belong praise and thanksgiving!

My prayer for you as you read this book is for God to bless you, for you to experience healing from the greatest physician of all, Jesus Christ; and like me, may you walk by faith!"

Healing Prayers

Dear reader, I hope by now the Holy Spirit has convinced you that healing is available for you through the atoning death of Jesus at the Cross. I hope you are convinced as well that as a child of God, you can release the healing of the kingdom of God to those that are sick and suffering with sickness and disease. This is part of His purpose for your life: for you to be an instrument of healing and life in this planet. Rise up, in the power of the Holy Spirit, and possess your inheritance of healing; to be healed and to heal is part of the glorious gospel of the kingdom! If you neglect this aspect of your inheritance, there will be a vacuum created, and the enemy will step in to possess it with counterfeit gifts of healings to deceive many. It's already happening across our nation! Let's stand up for Jesus and release His mercy and compassion to a sick and dying world!

Prayer for Salvation:

"Father, I come before You now repenting for my sins. Lord Jesus, I believe You are the Son of God. I believe that You died for me on the Cross and that You paid the penalty for all my sin and iniquity. Cleanse me and wash me with Your precious blood and make me white as snow. I confess with my mouth what I believe in my heart: that Jesus is Lord and that God raised Him from the dead. I place my trust for my salvation on Your finished work on the Cross. Thank You, Jesus, for the gift of salvation and eternal life. Release Your Holy Spirit in me in a mighty way so that I can live in victory over sin, satan and the world. Lord Jesus, be glorified in my life. Amen."

Prayer for Healing:

"Lord Jesus, I believe that on the Cross you carried every sickness and disease so that I could be healed (Isaiah 53:4-5). Your Word says that "by Your stripes I have been healed" (1 Peter 2:24). Right now I give You my sickness and I receive Your healing.

Release the healing of Your kingdom into my body. I receive it by faith. I speak healing, health and restoration to my body. Thank You, Jesus, for healing me! Amen."

Prayer for Breaking of Curses:

"Lord Jesus, I thank You that You became a curse for me on the Cross (Galatians 3:13) so that I could be freed from the curse and be blessed instead. I repent for the sin that brought this curse on my family; I renounce it and I ask you for forgiveness. I break the curse and I nail it on the Cross. In the name of Jesus I break any demonic assignments attached to this curse. The blood of Jesus is more powerful than any curse in my family tree. Thank You, Lord, for Your abundant life. (Now pronounce the opposite of the curse, the blessing, over your life.)

Prayer of Forgiveness:

Heavenly Father, I thank You for forgiving me of all my sin. Thank You for cleansing me with the precious blood of Jesus. It is Your desire that now I forgive all who have hurt me or abused me in any way. I receive your grace right now in order to do so. In the name of Jesus, I now forgive _____ and I release _____ into the Father's hands. Lord, I ask you to bless _____ with your love, care and protection. I overcome evil with good. I speak blessings over _____'s life. I pray that _____ comes to know You personally. I give up any unforgiveness, bitterness, rage, anger and resentment in my heart. I give up any plans of revenge and retaliation. I want a clean heart. Lord create in me a pure heart, one that is pleasing in Your sight. Thank You, Jesus, for the grace to walk in forgiveness. Thank You for setting me free. Amen.

V

Healing Scriptures

"Death and life are in the power of the tongue,
And those who love it will eat its fruits." (Proverbs 18:21).

Because there is tremendous power in our words, for good or evil,
these are healing scriptures that you can establish over your life
or the life of a loved one. Something happens in the Spirit when
we start proclaiming the Word of God over a situation; He will
watch over His word to perform it (Jeremiah 1:12). He is the
"high priest of our confession" (Hebrews 3: 1); our confession
of the Scriptures are like "bombs" that we can drop through faith;
proclaiming, declaring, decreeing, and expecting the Lord to
intervene and release His blessing of healing. There is a shifting
that takes place in our spiritual atmosphere as we decree, declare
and proclaim His Word and not our fears. Let's start releasing
faith out of our mouths and not fear, for "without faith it is
impossible to please Him" (Hebrews 11:6). Fear attracts the
enemy; faith kicks fear out of the way. In addition, as we "hear"
the Word of God again and again, our minds are renewed and we
will have greater faith for healing, for "faith comes by hearing…."
(Romans 10:17)

Genesis 20: 17
"Then Abraham prayed to God; and God healed Abimelech, and
also healed his wife and female slaves so that they bore children."

Exodus 15:26:
"If you will diligently hearken to the voice of the Lord your
God, and do that which is right in His eyes, and give heed to His

commandments and keep all His statutes, I will put none of the diseases upon you which I put upon the Egyptians; for I am the Lord your healer."

Exodus 23:25-26
"You shall serve the Lord your God, and I will bless your bread and your water; and I will take sickness away from the midst of you. None shall cast her young or be barren in your land; I will fulfill the number of your days."

Deuteronomy 7: 15
"And the lord will take away from you all sickness; and none of the evil diseases of Egypt, which you knew, will He inflict upon you, but He will lay them upon all who hate you."

Psalm 91: 9-10
"Because you have made the Lord your refuge, the Most High your habitation, no evil shall befall you, no scourge come near your tent."

Psalm 103: 2-3
"Bless the Lord, O my soul, and forget not all His benefits, who forgives all your iniquity, who heals all your diseases."

Psalm 107: 20
"...He sent forth His word, and healed them, and delivered them from destruction."

Psalm 118: 17
"I shall not die, but I shall live, and recount the deeds of the Lord."

Psalm 119: 107
"I am sorely afflicted; give me life, O Lord, according to Thy word."

Proverbs 3: 1-2
"My son, do not forget my teaching, but let your heart keep my commandments; for length of days and years of life and abundant welfare will they give you."

Proverbs 3: 7-8
"Be not wise in your own eyes; fear the Lord, and turn away from evil. It will be healing to your flesh and refreshment to your bones."

Proverbs 4: 20-23
"My son, be attentive to My words; incline your ear to my saying. Let them not escape from your sight; keep them within your heart. For they are life to him who finds them, and healing to all his flesh."

Proverbs 10: 27
" The fear of the Lord prolongs life, but the years of the wicked will be short."

Proverbs 12: 18(b)
"...the tongue of the wise brings healing."

Proverbs 14:30
"A tranquil mind gives life to the flesh...."

Proverbs 15: 30
"The light of the eyes rejoices the heart, and good news refreshes the bones."

Proverbs 16:24
"Pleasant words are like a honeycomb, sweetness to the soul and health to the body."

Proverbs 18:21
"Death and life are in the power of the tongue, and those who love

it will eat its fruits."

Proverbs 19: 23
"The fear of the Lord leads to life; and he who has it rests satisfied; he will not be visited by harm."

Proverbs 28: 13
"He who conceals his transgressions will not prosper, but he who confesses and forsakes them will obtain mercy."

Isaiah 35: 5-6
"Then the eyes of the blind shall be opened, and the ears of the deaf unstopped; then shall the lame man leap like a hart, and the tongues of the dumb sing for joy."

Isaiah 53: 4-5
"Yet it was our infirmities that He bore, our sufferings that He endured, while we thought of Him as stricken, as one smitten by God and afflicted. But He was pierced for our offenses, crushed for our sins, upon Him was the chastisement that makes us whole, by His stripes we were healed." (NAB).

Isaiah 58: 11
"And the Lord will guide you continually, and satisfy your desire with good things, and make your bones strong; and you shall be like a watered garden, like a spring of water, whose waters fail not."

Jeremiah 30: 17
"For I will restore health to you, and your wounds I will heal, says the Lord...."

Jeremiah 33: 6
"Behold, I will bring to it health and healing, and I will heal them and reveal to them abundance of prosperity and security."

Ezekiel 34: 15-16
"I Myself will be the shepherd of My sheep, and I will make
them lie down," says the Lord God. "I will seek the lost, and I
will bring back the strayed, and I will bind up the crippled, and I
will strengthen the weak, and the fat and the strong I will watch
over...."

Joel 3: 10
"...Let the weak say, I am strong." (NKJ).

Matthew 4: 23-24
"And He went about all Galilee, teaching in their synagogues and
preaching the gospel of the kingdom and healing every disease and
every infirmity among the people. So His fame spread throughout
all Syria, and they brought Him all the sick, those afflicted with
various diseases and pains, demoniacs, epileptics, and paralytics,
and He healed them."

Matthew 8: 2-3
"...and behold, a leper came to Him and knelt before Him, saying,
"Lord, if you will, you can make me clean.' And He stretched
out His hand and touched him, saying, 'I will; be clean.' And
immediately his leprosy was cleansed."

Matthew 8: 5-7
"As He entered Capernaum, a centurion came forward to Him,
beseeching Him and saying, 'Lord, my servant is lying paralyzed
at home, in terrible distress.' And He said to him, 'I will come and
heal him.'"

Matthew 8: 14-15
"And when Jesus entered Peter's house, He saw his mother-in-law
lying sick with a fever; He touched her hand, and the fever left her,
and she rose and served him."

Healing is for You!

Matthew 8: 16-17
"That evening they brought to Him many who were possessed with
demons; and He cast out the spirits with a word, and healed all
who were sick. This was to fulfill what was spoken by the prophet
Isaiah, 'He took our infirmities and bore our diseases.'"

Matthew 9: 2
"And behold, they brought to Him a paralytic, lying on his bed;
and when Jesus saw their faith He said to the paralytic, 'Take heart,
my son; your sins are forgiven.'"

Matthew 9: 20-22
"And behold, a woman who had suffered from a hemorrhage for
twelve years came up behind Him and touched the fringe of His
garment; for she said to herself, 'If I only touch His garment, I
shall be made well.' Jesus turned, and seeing her He said 'Take
heart, daughter; your faith has made you well.' And instantly the
woman was made well."

Matthew 9: 28-30
"When He entered the house, the blind men came to Him; and
Jesus said to them, 'Do you believe that I am able to do this?'
They said to Him, 'Yes, Lord.' Then He touched their eyes,
saying, 'According to your faith be it done to you.' And their eyes
were opened."

Matthew 9:35-36
"And Jesus went about all the cities and villages, teaching in their
synagogues and preaching the gospel of the kingdom, and healing
every disease and every infirmity. When He saw the crowds, He
had compassion for them, because they were harassed and helpless,
like sheep without a shepherd."

Matthew 10: 1
"And He called to Him His twelve disciples and gave them

authority over unclean spirits, to cast them out, and to heal every
disease and every infirmity."

Matthew 10: 7-8
"And preach as you go, saying, 'The kingdom of heaven is at
hand.' Heal the sick, raise the dead, cleanse lepers, cast out
demons. You received without pay, give without pay."

Matthew 14:14
"As He went ashore He saw a great throng; and He had
compassion on them, and healed their sick."

Matthew 14: 35-36
"And when the men of that place recognized Him, they sent
round to all that region and brought to Him all that were sick, and
besought Him that they night only touch the fringe of His garment;
and as many as touched it were made well."

Matthew 15: 28
"Then Jesus answered her, 'O woman, great is your faith! Be
it done for you as you desire.' And her daughter was healed
instantly."

Matthew 15:30-31
"And great crowds came to Him, bringing with them the lame, the
maimed, the blind, the dumb, and many others, and they put them
at His feet, and He healed them, so that the throng wondered, when
they saw the dumb speaking, the maimed whole, the lame walking,
and the blind seeing; and they glorified the God of Israel."

Matthew 21: 14
"And the blind and the lame came to Him in the temple, and He
healed them."

Mark 3: 5
"...and said to the man, 'Stretch out your hand.' He stretched it out, and his hand was restored."

Mark 3: 9
"And He told His disciples to have a boat ready for Him because of the crowd, lest they should crush Him; for He had healed any, so that all who had diseases pressed upon Him to touch Him."

Mark 6: 12-13
"So they went out and preached that men should repent. And they cast out many demons, and anointed with oil many that were sick and healed them."

Mark 7: 32-35
"And they brought to Him a man who was deaf and had an impediment in his speech; and they besought Him to lay His hand upon him. And taking him aside from the multitude privately, He put His fingers into his ears, and He spat and touched his tongue; and looking up to heaven, He sighed, and said to him, 'Ephphatha,' that is, 'Be opened.' And his ears were opened, his tongue was released, and he spoke plainly."

Mark 10: 51-52
"And Jesus said to him, 'What do you want me to do for you?' And the blind man said to him, 'Master, let me receive my sight.' And Jesus said to him, 'Go your way; your faith has made you well.' And immediately he received his sight and followed Him on the way."

Mark 16: 17-18
"And these signs will accompany those who believe; in my name they will cast out demons; they will speak in new tongues; they will pick up serpents, and if they drink any deadly thing, it will

not hurt them; they will lay their hands on the sick, and they will recover."

Luke 5: 15
"...and great multitudes gathered to hear and to be healed of their infirmities."

Luke 6:17-18
"...who came to hear Him and be healed of their diseases; and those who were troubled with unclean spirits were cure. And all the crowd sought to touch Him, for power came forth from Him and healed them all."

Luke 7: 13-15
"And when the Lord saw her, He had compassion on her and said to her, 'Do not weep.' And He came and touched the bier, and the bearers stood still. And He said, 'Young man, I say to you, arise.' And the dead man sat up, and began to speak. And He gave him to his mother."

Luke 7: 21-22
"In that hour He cured many of diseases and plagues and evil spirits, and on many that were blind He bestowed sight. And He answered them, 'Go and tell John what you have seen and heard; the blind receive their sight, the lame walk, lepers are cleansed, and the deaf hear, the dead are raised up, the poor have good news preached to them.'"

Luke 9: 1-2
"And He called the twelve together and gave them power and authority over all demons and to cure disease, and He sent them out ot preach the kingdom of God and to heal."

Healing is for You!

Luke 10:8
"Whenever you enter a town and they receive you, eat what is set before you; heal the sick in it and say to them, 'The kingdom of God has come near to you.'"

Luke 13: 12-13
"And when Jesus saw her, He called her and said to her, 'Woman, you are freed from your infirmity. And He laid His hands upon her, and immediately she was made straight, and she praised God.'"

Luke 17:12-14
"And as He entered a village, He was met by ten lepers, who stood at a distance and lifted up their voices and said, 'Jesus, Master, have mercy on us.' When He saw them He said to them, 'Go and show yourselves to the priests.' And as they went they were cleansed."

Luke 22:43
"And there appeared to Him an angel from heaven, strengthening him."

Luke 22:50-51
"And one of them struck the slave of the high priest and cut off his right ear. But Jesus said, 'No more of this!' And He touched his ear and healed him."

John 4:50-51
"Jesus said to him, 'Go, your son will live.' The man believed the word that Jesus spoke to him and went his way. As he was going down, his servants met him and told him that his son was living."

John 5:8-9
"Jesus said to him, 'Rise take up your pallet, and walk.' And at once the man was healed, and he took up his pallet and walked."

John 9: 6-7
"As He said this, He spat on the ground and made clay of the spittle and anointed the man's eyes with the clay saying to him, 'Go, was in the pool of Siloam' (which means Sent). So he went and washed and came back seeing."

John 11: 43-44
"When He had said this, He cried with a loud voice, 'Lazarus, come out.' The dead man came out, his hands and feet bound with bandages, and his face wrapped with a cloth. Jesus said to them, 'Unbind him, and let him go.'"

Acts 3: 6-10
"But Peter said, 'I have no silver and gold, but I give you what I have; in the name of Jesus Christ of Nazareth, walk.' And he took him by the right hand and raised him up; and immediately his feet and ankles were made strong. And leaping up he stood and walked and entered the temple with them, walking and leaping and praising God."

Acts 4: 29
"And now, Lord, look upon their threats, and grant to thy servants to speak thy word with all boldness, while thou stretchest out thy hand to heal, and signs and wonders are performed through the name of they holy servant Jesus."

Acts 5: 12
"Now many signs and wonders were done among the people by the hands of the apostles."

Acts 5: 14-16
"And more than ever believers were added to the Lord, multitudes both of men and women, so that they even carried out the sick into the streets, and laid them on beds and pallets, that as Peter came by at least his shadow might fall on some of them. The people also

gathered from the towns around Jerusalem, bringing the sick and those afflicted with unclean spirits, and they were all healed."

Acts 6: 8
"And Stephen, full of grace and power, did great wonders and signs among the people."

Acts 8: 6-8
"And the multitudes with one accord gave heed to what was said by Philip, when they heard him and saw the signs which he did. For unclean spirits came out of many who were possessed, crying with a loud voice; and many who were paralyzed or lame were healed. So there was much joy in that city."

Acts 9: 34-35
"And Peter said to him, 'Aeneas, Jesus Christ heals you; rise and make your bed.' And immediately he rose. And all the residents of Lydda and Sharon saw him, and they turned to the Lord."

Acts 9: 40
"But Peter put them all outside and knelt down and prayed; then turning to the body he said, 'Tabitha, rise.' And she opened her eyes, and when she saw Peter she sat up."

Acts 14: 9-10
"He listened to Paul speaking; and Paul, looking intently at him and seeing that he had faith to be made well, said in a loud voice, 'Stand upright on your feet.' And he sprang up and walked."

Acts 19: 11-12
"And God did extraordinary miracles by the hands of Paul, so that handkerchiefs or aprons were carried away from his body to the sick and diseases left them and the evil spirits came out of them."

Healing Scriptures

Romans 8: 2
"For the law of the Spirit of life in Christ Jesus has set me free from the lawof sin and death."

Romans 8: 11
"If the Spirit of Him who raised Jesus from the dead dwells in you, He who raised Christ Jesus from the dead will give life to your mortal bodies also through His Spirit who dwells in you."

Galatians 3: 13-14
"Christ redeemed us from the curse of the law, having become a curse for us—for it is written, 'Cursed be every one who hangs on a tree'—that in Christ Jesus the blessing of Abraham might come upon the Gentiles...."

James 13: 14-16
"Is any among you sick? Let him call for the elders of the church, and let them pray over him, anointing him with oil in the name of the Lord; and the prayer of faith will save the sick man, and the Lord will raise him up; and if he has committed sins, he will be forgiven. Therefore confess your sins to one another, and pray for one another, that you may be healed. The prayer of a righteous man has great power in its effects."

1 Peter 2: 24
"He Himself bore our sins in his body on the tree, that we might die to sin and live to righteousness. By His wounds you have been healed."

3 John 2
"Beloved, I pray that all may go well with you and that you may be in health; I know that it is well with your soul."